MAYER SMITH

The Dragon Queen's Forbidden Consort

Copyright © 2025 by Mayer Smith

All rights reserved. No part of this publication may be reproduced, stored or transmitted in any form or by any means, electronic, mechanical, photocopying, recording, scanning, or otherwise without written permission from the publisher. It is illegal to copy this book, post it to a website, or distribute it by any other means without permission.

This novel is entirely a work of fiction. The names, characters and incidents portrayed in it are the work of the author's imagination. Any resemblance to actual persons, living or dead, events or localities is entirely coincidental.

Mayer Smith asserts the moral right to be identified as the author of this work.

Mayer Smith has no responsibility for the persistence or accuracy of URLs for external or third-party Internet Websites referred to in this publication and does not guarantee that any content on such Websites is, or will remain, accurate or appropriate.

Designations used by companies to distinguish their products are often claimed as trademarks. All brand names and product names used in this book and on its cover are trade names, service marks, trademarks and registered trademarks of their respective owners. The publishers and the book are not associated with any product or vendor mentioned in this book. None of the companies referenced within the book have endorsed the book.

First edition

*This book was professionally typeset on Reedsy.
Find out more at reedsy.com*

Contents

1	A Throne Won in Blood	1
2	The Last Dragon Prince	8
3	A Warrior's Heart, A Queen's Duty	12
4	An Offer of Chains	19
5	Whispers of Rebellion	26
6	The Unspoken Pact	34
7	A Consort's Betrayal	40
8	To Trust a Foe	48
9	A Queen's Secret Desire	55
10	Flames of the Past	63
11	The War Council's Demand	70
12	A Forbidden Alliance	77
13	The Shadowed Oath	85
14	A Kingdom Divided	93
15	Beneath Dragon Wings	101
16	A Queen's Betrayal	108
17	The Consort's Vow	115
18	The Battle of Fire and Blood	122
19	The Price of Love	130
20	The Rise of the Dragon Queen	137

One

A Throne Won in Blood

The acrid stench of burning flesh clung to the air, mingling with the metallic tang of spilled blood. Smoke coiled through the ruins of the royal hall, curling its blackened fingers around shattered columns and corpses alike. The battle had ended, but the echoes of death still whispered through the broken stones.

Kaelith stood at the center of it all, sword in hand, blood dripping from the curved blade. Her armor bore deep gouges, her left pauldron missing entirely, exposing a gash that cut from her shoulder down to her bicep. The pain was a dull throb, swallowed by the rush of adrenaline still pumping through her veins.

She could hear the crackling flames consuming the banners of the old queen—her mother. Once proud crimson and gold, they now disintegrated into curling embers that danced in the night.

The throne room was unrecognizable. The great glass skylight had shattered during the siege, the pieces reflecting the dying torchlight like scattered diamonds. The polished marble floor, once an expanse of pristine white, was smeared with gore. Bodies of her mother's guards lay strewn about, their weapons pried from lifeless hands.

Kaelith let out a slow breath. The battle was over.

The war had just begun.

A pair of boots crunched over the debris behind her. She turned her head slightly, not lowering her sword.

"My queen."

The voice belonged to General Varek, a mountain of a man with a scar running from his jawline to his temple. He knelt at her side, blood staining his breastplate. His sword, still slick from battle, rested at his hip.

"The palace is ours. The last of the queen's loyalists have either fallen or fled. You stand alone as ruler."

Kaelith's grip on her sword tightened. She had fought for this moment, had bled for it. Yet, staring at the throne—her mother's throne—she felt none of the triumph she had expected.

Only the weight of the crown yet to be placed upon her head.

"She never saw it coming," Varek mused, his gaze flickering to the corpse slumped against the dais.

Kaelith's eyes followed.

Queen Elira of Veyrith lay where she had fallen, her once-imposing figure reduced to a heap of ruined silk and shattered pride. The dagger Kaelith had driven into her chest still remained, its jeweled hilt glinting mockingly. The queen's unseeing eyes were frozen in disbelief, her lips parted as if she had died mid-protest.

A mother killed by her own daughter.

Kaelith had expected more resistance. She had prepared for it. She had envisioned a final duel, an epic confrontation where her mother would wield her blade with the ferocity of a lioness protecting her reign. Instead, Elira had barely lifted a hand to defend herself.

She had only whispered, "I should have killed you first."

Even now, the words curdled in Kaelith's stomach.

Varek studied her face. "Regret?"

"No," Kaelith said. "Just unfinished business."

Varek nodded, satisfied. "Then finish it, my queen."

He gestured to the throne.

Kaelith forced her feet forward, stepping over the lifeless guards who had once sworn to protect her mother. Each step felt heavier than the last. When she reached the throne, she lifted her gaze to the massive banners hanging above it—symbols of the dragon-blooded kingdom Veyrith had conquered and erased from history.

The dragons had burned. Their people had been slaughtered. And the last heir to the throne of Rhaedros had been dragged in chains to kneel before Queen Elira.

Now, as Kaelith turned, she saw him again.

The guards dragged the prisoner through the blood-soaked hall, his wrists bound in irons, his face shadowed beneath the matted strands of his dark hair. His tunic was torn, revealing scars that crisscrossed his body like a cruel map of survival. He was taller than she remembered, broader. But his eyes—those golden, burning eyes—were still the same.

Prince Rhyzor of Rhaedros.

The last dragon heir.

The boy she had once loved.

He had been captured before the battle, found lurking in the shadows of the city like a phantom of vengeance. The men who had seized him had not recognized him at first, but Kaelith had.

The moment she had heard his name, something in her had turned to ice.

Now he stood before her, silent, unmoving, his eyes fixed on hers.

"Rhyzor of Rhaedros," General Varek intoned, stepping forward. "You were found trespassing in the capital, conspiring against the crown. By rights, you should be executed at dawn."

Kaelith kept her face unreadable.

The warrior in her knew what had to be done. The queen in her knew it was a risk to let him live.

But the girl she used to be, the one who had once kissed him beneath the shadow of the old oaks, whispered something else entirely.

Rhyzor tilted his chin, his jaw tight. "Then kill me."

The silence in the throne room was deafening.

Kaelith stepped down from the dais. Her boots echoed against the stone as she moved toward him, stopping just a breath away. She reached out—not for a blade, but for his face. The guards tensed, but she ignored them.

Her fingers brushed against his bruised cheek.

He did not flinch.

She studied him, the flicker of something unspoken passing between them.

Then she stepped back.

"No," she said at last, her voice quiet but sharp as steel.

Varek frowned. "My queen—"

Kaelith cut him off with a glance.

"Chain him," she ordered. "But do not kill him."

Rhyzor's lips curled in something close to a smirk, though his eyes remained cold. "Afraid, Kaelith?"

She met his gaze, unblinking. "No. I just have other plans for you."

She turned before he could speak again, making her way back to the throne. She could feel Varek's disapproval burning into her back, the unease rippling through the gathered warriors.

Let them question her.

Let them wonder why she would spare the last dragon prince.

For Kaelith did not yet know the answer herself.

All she knew was this:

The war was not over.

It was just beginning.

Two

The Last Dragon Prince

The dungeon reeked of damp stone, stale blood, and something more insidious—despair.

Torchlight flickered along the cold walls, casting jagged shadows that stretched and writhed like trapped souls. Chains rattled with each movement, the metal scraping against the stone as the prisoner shifted. He did not cry out, nor did he beg for mercy. Instead, he sat in eerie silence, his back straight despite the wounds that marred his flesh, his golden eyes gleaming like embers in the dark.

Prince Rhyzor of Rhaedros did not belong in a cage.

Yet here he was, shackled like an animal in the bowels of the kingdom that had murdered his people.

Kaelith stood just outside his cell, her gloved fingers curling around the iron bars. The torches lining the corridor barely reached him, leaving him in half-shadow, but she could see him well enough. His clothes were torn, his dark hair unkempt, and blood crusted along his temple where a fresh wound had not yet healed.

Still, he watched her with quiet defiance, unmoved by the chains biting into his wrists.

"Do you find this amusing?" Kaelith's voice cut through the damp air like a blade.

Rhyzor tilted his head, his smirk slow and deliberate. "I find it predictable."

She narrowed her eyes. "You think I brought you here to gloat?"

"I think you don't know why you brought me here at all." His voice was smooth, unshaken, carrying none of the bitterness she expected. It unnerved her more than hatred would have.

Kaelith inhaled slowly, forcing herself to remain composed. He was not wrong. She should have ordered his execution. She should have ended this war before it had a chance to breathe again.

And yet…

"You were a fool to come back to Veyrith," she said, her grip tightening on the bars. "Did you really think you could strike from the shadows and walk away unscathed?"

Rhyzor let out a quiet chuckle. "I never intended to walk away."

Something in his voice sent a chill through her. He was waiting for something—some opportunity she had not yet seen.

She glanced at the guards stationed behind her. They stood at attention, their hands on their weapons, but Rhyzor hadn't so much as lifted a finger in resistance. He was biding his time.

Kaelith stepped closer, lowering her voice. "Are you waiting for them?"

Rhyzor's expression did not change, but something flickered behind his eyes.

"Who?" he asked smoothly.

She ignored the lie. "You didn't come here alone."

Silence stretched between them.

Then—

"You always were perceptive," he murmured.

Kaelith's pulse quickened.

The thought had nagged at her since the moment they captured him. The last dragon prince would not have returned to the city of his enemies without a plan. He would not have walked into their clutches willingly—unless there was more to his surrender than she had realized.

A distraction.

Her blood ran cold.

"How many?" she demanded.

Rhyzor smiled, slow and infuriating. "Does it matter?"

Kaelith turned sharply on her heel. "Double the guards at the gates," she ordered the nearest soldier. "No one enters or leaves without my command."

The man bowed and hurried off, his footsteps echoing through the corridor.

When she turned back, she found Rhyzor watching her with something dangerously close to amusement.

"Afraid, Kaelith?" he asked, mocking her the way he had when they were children, when the war had not yet turned them into enemies.

She hated the way he spoke her name. Not as a title, not as an insult, but as something *familiar*.

She pushed past it. "If you think your people will save you,

you are mistaken."

He leaned forward, the dim light catching the sharp angles of his face. "And if you think I need saving, *you* are mistaken."

His chains rattled as he shifted, the iron digging into his wrists. His golden eyes burned in the torchlight, the same fire that had once set her heart ablaze now sending an unease curling through her chest.

Rhyzor was dangerous.

Not just because he was the last of the dragon-blooded.

Not just because he was a warrior.

But because he knew her.

He knew the girl she used to be.

The girl who had once loved him.

Kaelith forced herself to harden. "Tomorrow at dawn, I will decide your fate."

Rhyzor smirked, as if he already knew what her decision would be.

And that frightened her more than anything.

She turned, her boots striking against the stone as she walked away, the heavy doors slamming shut behind her.

But even as she ascended from the dungeons into the halls of her newly claimed throne, she could still feel his gaze on her.

Watching.

Waiting.

For what, she did not know.

But something told her she would soon find out.

Three

A Warrior's Heart, A Queen's Duty

The council chamber was filled with the scent of burning cedar and the murmur of dissenting voices. Flickering candlelight cast long shadows across the circular table, where Veyrith's warlords, generals, and high-ranking nobles had gathered in the wake of Kaelith's victory. The air was thick with tension, a silent battle waging within the chamber that had nothing to do with swords.

Kaelith sat at the head of the table, her newly claimed crown resting on her brow, the weight of it pressing heavier than she expected. Her fingers drummed against the polished wood, a habit she had never broken, despite the years of discipline drilled into her.

They were arguing over him.

Rhyzor.

"The dragon prince should be executed at once," barked Lord Jeren, his heavily ringed hand slamming against the table. His grizzled beard twitched with every word, his deep-set eyes glinting with anger. "His existence alone is an act of defiance against your rule."

General Varek, seated to her right, let out a low hum. "An execution would be the most prudent course of action, my queen. It would end the whispers of rebellion before they fester."

"And yet," Kaelith said, her voice even, "the last time a dragon prince was slaughtered, his people burned half this kingdom to the ground in retaliation."

Silence.

She let it stretch, let them taste the weight of their own bloodstained history.

Lord Jeren scowled. "That was years ago—his people are gone."

"They are not gone," she countered smoothly. "They are in hiding. Scattered, waiting." Her gaze swept across the table. "If we make a martyr of him, we invite war."

"Then let it come," another noble, Lord Cailan, muttered.

Kaelith exhaled sharply. "Let me be clear: I did not fight for this throne only to bring another war to its doorstep." She leaned forward. "Do you doubt my strength?"

Silence again. This time, thicker.

"No, my queen," Jeren said at last, though his tone was reluctant.

She had killed her own mother for this throne. They knew better than to question her resolve.

Still, the doubt lingered like a shadow in the candlelight.

General Varek cleared his throat. "Then what will you do with him?"

The question hovered in the air, waiting.

She had not yet decided.

Rhyzor was a complication she had not accounted for. A ghost from the past that should have been buried alongside the ashes of his kingdom.

She had ordered him shackled, but not dead.

Now she had to live with that choice.

Kaelith straightened. "He will remain imprisoned until I decide otherwise."

Murmurs. Discontented, but restrained.

"And if his people come for him?" Lord Cailan pressed.

Kaelith's gaze darkened. "Then we will be ready."

It was the only answer they would get from her tonight.

She rose, the weight of her armor shifting with her. The room quieted as she did, and without another word, she turned and left.

The torches along the dungeon corridor flickered as Kaelith descended the stone steps, the air growing colder with each step. The guards stationed outside the iron-barred cell straightened as she approached.

"Leave us," she ordered.

They hesitated only for a moment before bowing and stepping away, leaving her alone with him.

Rhyzor sat against the far wall, his wrists still bound in iron, though his posture was too relaxed for a man in chains. He looked up at her through the mess of his dark hair, the golden hue of his eyes catching the torchlight.

For a long moment, neither spoke.

Then—

"You came." His voice was rough, but not with weakness.

"I had little choice." She stepped forward, her boots echoing against the stone. "It seems you have become quite the problem."

His lips quirked. "I always was."

Kaelith crossed her arms. "You should be dead."

"Yet here I am."

His unflinching gaze unsettled her more than she wanted to admit.

"Why did you return?" she demanded.

Rhyzor leaned his head back against the stone. "You already know."

Kaelith clenched her jaw. "Say it."

He exhaled, a slow, measured breath. "Vengeance."

The word sent a chill through her, though she did not let it show.

"I should have expected nothing less."

He watched her carefully. "What will you do with me, Kaelith?"

The sound of her name on his tongue made something flicker in her chest. A memory—of stolen moments in sunlit glades, of whispered promises that never came to be.

She pushed it aside.

"I do not know," she admitted.

He raised a brow. "That is unlike you."

She hated how well he still knew her.

Kaelith stepped closer, gripping the iron bars. "You had a chance to kill me. You didn't take it."

Rhyzor's expression remained unreadable. "Neither did you."

Silence stretched between them, filled with unspoken things.

Finally, she said, "Do you regret it?"

His smirk returned, sharp as a dagger. "I never regret unfinished business."

Kaelith let out a slow breath. "Neither do I."

Then she turned, leaving him behind.

But as she ascended the stairs, his voice followed her—low, steady, and laced with something dangerous.

"This is not over, Kaelith."

She did not look back.

Because she knew he was right.

Four

An Offer of Chains

~~~
~~~

The great hall of the palace was nearly silent, save for the slow crackling of the torches lining the walls. Shadows stretched long and jagged over the polished marble floor, the glow of the flames licking across the banners that hung above the dais—the sigil of the conquered dragon kingdom still woven into the fabric, a mockery of a people that once ruled the skies.

Kaelith stood at the top of the dais, facing the gathered council, her face a mask of control. At her feet, the throne loomed—tall, imposing, yet strangely empty.

She did not sit.

To sit was to accept, to bow to the demands of the men who circled her like vultures. She had not fought for this throne to be ruled by those who whispered in its shadows.

At the center of the room, kneeling with his hands bound in chains, was the last dragon prince.

Rhyzor.

The man they all wanted dead.

The man she could not bring herself to kill.

"Your Majesty," Lord Jeren spoke first, his voice edged with impatience. "You summoned us for a decision. Let it be made."

Kaelith let the silence stretch, let it press against their skin like the weight of a storm.

Then, she descended the steps, each footstep echoing in the hush.

She did not stop until she was only a breath away from Rhyzor, the scent of blood and smoke clinging to him, his golden eyes locked onto hers.

A dangerous gaze. Not desperate. Not broken.

Watching. Waiting.

She knelt before him, the entire court holding their breath.

And then she spoke.

"You swore vengeance against this throne," she said.

His smirk was slow, deliberate. "And I still do."

A murmur rippled through the nobles. Kaelith did not look away.

"Then tell me," she said, tilting her head slightly. "If I were to free you now, what would you do?"

Rhyzor's chains clinked as he shifted, but he did not hesitate.

"I would finish what I started."

There was no lie in his voice.

The murmurs grew louder, Lord Jeren stepping forward. "My queen, this is madness. He is a traitor, an enemy to the crown. He should be executed at once."

Kaelith did not break her gaze from Rhyzor's. "And yet, he lives."

A flicker of something unreadable passed through his eyes.

"I could kill you right now," she said softly.

Rhyzor smirked. "Then why haven't you?"

The question coiled around her like a whisper from the past.

She had asked herself the same thing a hundred times since his capture.

She did not look away.

Instead, she stood, her voice sharp as steel.

"I will not execute him."

The uproar was instant.

Shouts of protest, of outrage, of disbelief. The council erupted into argument, half rising from their seats.

Kaelith let them.

She let the chaos swell, let the fire in their voices rise—until she slammed her blade into the marble floor.

The sound was deafening.

The silence that followed was even louder.

She lifted her chin. "You call for war when we have only just won the last one." Her gaze swept over them, sharp and unyielding. "If we execute him, we invite another. His death does not erase his people. His death does not end their vengeance. It only fuels it."

Lord Cailan, a younger noble with calculating eyes, frowned. "Then what do you propose, my queen?"

An Offer of Chains

Kaelith turned back to Rhyzor.

Slowly, deliberately, she reached for the key at her belt.

And unlocked his chains.

A sharp intake of breath ran through the court.

Rhyzor did not move.

She leaned closer. "You are mine now."

His golden eyes flickered, unreadable.

"The last of your kind," she continued, voice steady. "A prince of a dead kingdom. A warrior with no army. You belong to no one." She paused. "Unless you choose to belong to me."

Silence.

Lord Jeren's face was red with fury. "You cannot mean to—"

"I do." She turned to the council, lifting her chin. "He will serve as my guard."

Outrage.

More shouts.

"Impossible!"

"He will kill you in your sleep!"

"You are gambling with the future of Veyrith!"

Kaelith raised a hand. The voices fell to uneasy murmurs.

"If he kills me," she said, voice quiet but certain, "then I was not strong enough to be queen."

She turned back to Rhyzor.

And extended her hand.

The chains lay at his feet, his wrists now free. He could reach for her. He could strike her down.

Instead, he looked at her—truly looked at her.

And then, after a long moment, he smirked.

Slowly, he reached forward—

And took her hand.

A gasp rippled through the court.

Kaelith pulled him to his feet, standing close enough that she could feel the warmth of his skin beneath the grime of battle, could see the ghost of the boy she had once known in the man before her now.

Rhyzor's voice was soft, dangerous. "You play a dangerous game, Kaelith."

She smiled.

"I always have."

Five

Whispers of Rebellion

The torches lining the palace halls flickered, their golden glow doing little to push back the thick shadows clinging to the stone walls. The air carried the scent of damp stone, iron, and something more elusive—the tension of a kingdom on the edge of unrest.

Kaelith walked with measured steps, her cloak trailing behind her as she descended the narrow passage leading to her war chambers. The echoes of her boots against the marble floor followed her like ghostly footsteps. Outside, the city was restless, a pulse of unease spreading through the streets like a slow-burning fire.

The people had not forgotten the blood that stained the throne.

Nor had they forgotten the dragon prince in chains.

She had expected discontent. A ruler who took the throne by force could not expect devotion overnight. But the whispers had grown louder. Murmurs of rebellion, of dissatisfaction, of old enemies still lurking in the shadows.

And she knew exactly where those whispers had begun.

She pushed open the heavy wooden doors of the war chamber, stepping inside. The long table stretched before her, scattered with maps, old treaties, and fresh reports. Seated around it were her council—men who had once advised her mother, men who now struggled to understand the ruler that had taken her place.

Lord Jeren was already standing, his expression twisted with poorly veiled frustration. "My queen, we cannot ignore this any longer."

Kaelith shut the door behind her. "Then do not waste my time with dramatics. Speak plainly."

Jeren's lips pressed into a thin line. "The people are not pleased."

"That much is clear."

General Varek, ever composed, leaned forward. "The city is uneasy. They question your decision to spare the dragon prince." His dark eyes flickered to her, careful, searching. "And your decision to keep him so close."

Kaelith felt the weight of their unspoken accusations settle on her shoulders.

She had expected resistance when she had chosen to bind Rhyzor to her service instead of executing him. Expected it from the nobles, from the council, from the very men who had fought to see his people destroyed.

What she had not expected was the fear.

"They believe I have made a mistake," she said coolly.

"They believe you have betrayed the kingdom," Lord Cailan corrected, his tone edged with warning.

The words settled between them like a blade between the ribs.

Kaelith let out a slow breath. "Have I?"

Silence.

She turned her gaze on each of them, watching, waiting.

It was Jeren who finally broke it. "The people do not understand your choice. And when they do not understand, they grow afraid."

"And afraid men seek new rulers," Cailan added.

The implication was clear.

Kaelith's grip tightened around the back of the chair. "There is no ruler but me."

"For now," Jeren muttered.

A dangerous statement.

Her fingers flexed against the wood, but her face remained unreadable. "Do you doubt my rule, Lord Jeren?"

He hesitated. Then, carefully, "No, my queen. But others might."

Kaelith turned away from them, walking toward the grand map that dominated the far wall. Her eyes traced the borders of Veyrith, the outlying regions, the strongholds still loyal to her banner.

She had taken the throne.

But keeping it would be another battle entirely.

"The rebellion is growing," Varek continued. "Not in open defiance, not yet. But the whispers are there. Some of your mother's loyalists remain in hiding. There are rumors of a leader among them—someone moving the pieces from the shadows."

Kaelith's gaze darkened. "A leader."

"Yes."

Her thoughts churned. There had been no clear heir after her mother's death—only the nobles who had sought to fill the void she had left behind. None had the strength to unite the opposition. Not alone.

But if someone had stepped forward…

"If a rebellion is forming, we must crush it before it takes root," Cailan said, his voice hard. "Find those responsible. End it before it begins."

It was the logical solution. The only one her generals would accept.

But Kaelith had spent too many years on the battlefield to believe that war was always the answer.

She turned back to the council. "If we kill them all, we become no better than the tyrants they fear."

"They do not fear you enough," Jeren snapped. "That is the problem."

Kaelith's jaw clenched.

She had ruled by the sword her entire life. But fear was a fickle thing—it inspired obedience, but never loyalty.

"I will deal with this," she said finally.

Cailan frowned. "How?"

Kaelith did not answer.

Because she already knew where she needed to go.

The training grounds were empty by the time she arrived, the torches casting long pools of light against the stone walls. The sounds of the city beyond the palace walls still echoed—distant voices, the occasional clang of metal, the hum of a restless kingdom.

At the center of the courtyard, Rhyzor stood with his arms crossed, his expression unreadable.

He was no longer bound in chains. No longer kneeling.

She had given him armor. A sword. Freedom within the walls of her own kingdom.

And yet, she could feel the tension rolling off him like a storm waiting to break.

Kaelith approached, stopping just a few paces away.

"You've heard the whispers," she said.

Rhyzor let out a low chuckle. "I'm surprised it took them this long."

Her eyes narrowed. "You sound amused."

He tilted his head. "You spared a man who should be dead. A man whose people still curse your throne. What did you expect?"

Kaelith inhaled slowly, forcing herself to remain calm. "I expected resistance. I did not expect a rebellion forming this quickly."

Rhyzor studied her. "And now you think I have something to do with it."

"I think you always have something to do with trouble."

His smirk was slow. "You always did know me too well."

She ignored the flicker of familiarity in his tone.

"This is not a game, Rhyzor," she said. "If there is a leader among the rebels, I need to find them before this escalates."

His golden eyes gleamed. "And you want my help."

Kaelith hesitated.

Asking him was a risk. A dangerous gamble.

But she had spent her life surrounded by men who followed orders out of fear.

Rhyzor, for all his defiance, had never been a man who bent so easily.

She needed someone who understood the rebels. Someone who knew the heart of vengeance better than anyone else.

She stepped closer.

"I need to know who's behind this," she said quietly. "I need to end this before it becomes war."

Rhyzor was silent for a long moment.

Then, finally, he sighed. "Very well."

Surprise flickered through her. "You'll help?"

His smirk returned. "I never said I would help."

He leaned in slightly, his voice low.

"I just want to see how this all plays out."

Kaelith's fists clenched, but she did not back down.

Because whether Rhyzor intended to help or not, one thing was certain—

The rebellion was coming.

And she had little time left to stop it.

Six

The Unspoken Pact

The night air was thick with the scent of damp stone and distant embers. Kaelith stood at the edge of the palace balcony, her hands gripping the cold marble railing as she gazed out over the restless city. The streets below pulsed with flickering torchlight, figures moving in the shadows like whispers come to life.

The rebellion was growing.

Not yet a fire, but smoldering embers, waiting for the right breath of air to ignite into something unstoppable.

She could feel it in the way the nobles whispered when she entered the council chamber. In the way her generals hesitated before answering her. In the way the people in the streets looked at the banners that hung from the palace walls—not with reverence, but with doubt.

And the doubt was spreading.

She inhaled slowly, steadying herself.

Behind her, the soft scuff of boots on stone announced his arrival before he spoke.

"You look troubled, Kaelith."

Rhyzor's voice was smooth, edged with something she couldn't quite place. Amusement, perhaps. Or calculation.

She did not turn. "You say that as if I am not always troubled."

He chuckled, stepping closer. "True."

She could feel his presence at her back, a warmth that clashed against the cold night air. He was close enough that she could hear the quiet creak of his leather armor, the way his breath was steady, measured.

She hated that she noticed.

"You still haven't decided," he said.

Kaelith closed her eyes briefly. "No."

"Then allow me to make it simple."

She finally turned to face him. His golden eyes glowed faintly in the torchlight, catching the fire in a way that made him look almost otherworldly.

A reminder of what he was.

What she had chosen to spare.

"What would you suggest, then?" she asked, her tone unreadable.

Rhyzor tilted his head. "You already know."

Silence stretched between them, thick with something unspoken.

Then—

"You need me."

Kaelith stiffened. "I need answers."

"And I'm the only one who can get them for you." He smirked. "That sounds like need to me."

Her jaw clenched. "I should have let you rot in that cell."

His smirk did not fade. "But you didn't."

Kaelith exhaled sharply, looking away.

The Unspoken Pact

She hated this. Hated the truth of his words. Hated that he was right.

She was running out of time.

The rebellion was not a distant threat—it was already here, moving in the shadows of her own kingdom. And Rhyzor, for all his arrogance, knew those shadows better than anyone.

She had two choices.

Crush the rebellion by force.

Or infiltrate it.

Neither option was without risk.

But only one of them gave her control over the inevitable war.

She turned back to him, her voice cold. "You would have me send you into the heart of the rebellion. And expect me to trust that you will not turn against me."

Rhyzor's smirk faded slightly, his gaze sharpening. "I expect you to do what you must to keep your throne."

Kaelith studied him carefully. "And why should I believe you won't betray me?"

He stepped closer, slow and deliberate, until there was almost no space between them.

His voice was quiet. "Because I have more to gain by staying alive."

Kaelith held his gaze, searching for deception.

She found none.

And that terrified her more than if he had lied.

She turned away, gripping the railing once more. "This is madness."

Rhyzor let out a low laugh. "Perhaps. But then, so is ruling."

The night wind brushed against her skin, carrying with it the distant hum of the city.

She hated that she had already made her decision.

Hated that she knew she would regret it.

But she was a queen before anything else.

And a queen did not flinch from difficult choices.

Kaelith exhaled slowly. "You will go."

Rhyzor's smirk returned. "I thought you'd never ask."

She turned to face him fully, her expression unreadable. "But understand this." She stepped closer, her voice lowering to a whisper. "If you betray me, I will not hesitate next time."

Rhyzor's golden eyes flickered with something unreadable.

Then, he smiled.

"I wouldn't expect anything less."

Kaelith turned away, her heart steady, her mind set.

The pact had been made.

Unspoken. Unbreakable.

And before the night was over, she knew—

The game had truly begun.

Seven

A Consort's Betrayal

The full moon hung low in the sky, its pale light spilling across the stone floors of the royal chambers. The air inside the room was thick with the scent of burning candles, their wax melting slowly, pooling around their bases. Kaelith stood before the grand mirror, her fingers grazing the edges of her crown, a crown that now seemed heavier than it ever had before. The weight of it felt different tonight. The weight of the throne had always been a burden, but now—now, it felt like a curse.

She had made her decision. She had spared him. Rhyzor. The last dragon prince. The enemy of her ancestors. The one man who had come closest to tearing her apart when they were children.

But she had made her choice.

And yet, here she stood—alone, staring at the reflection of a woman she didn't recognize.

The door creaked open behind her, and she didn't have to turn to know who it was. The air shifted with his presence.

"You're still awake," Rhyzor's voice broke the silence. It was low, almost a whisper, but there was an edge to it—a warning, perhaps.

Kaelith didn't respond at first. She simply kept her gaze fixed on the mirror, watching as her own reflection seemed to blur with the darkness beyond.

Rhyzor's footsteps were measured, the soft sound of his boots on the stone growing closer. She could feel his eyes on her, could feel the weight of his gaze even without looking.

"I told you I would return," he said softly.

She turned then, slowly, her eyes meeting his. The flames from the torches illuminated his face, casting sharp shadows that made his features seem even more chiseled than before. His dark hair was slightly tousled, and the faintest trace of a smile played at the corner of his lips. He stood just beyond the threshold, his posture relaxed, his arms crossed over his chest.

"Did you find what you were looking for?" Kaelith asked, her voice a mix of exhaustion and curiosity.

Rhyzor's eyes glinted, and for a moment, she saw something—

something that flickered behind the mask of confidence. A flicker of doubt, of hesitation.

"I found more than I expected," he replied, his voice tinged with something darker now.

Kaelith's heart skipped a beat, but she hid it beneath a veil of indifference. "What does that mean?"

Rhyzor stepped forward, his gaze never leaving hers. "It means that the rebellion is closer than we thought. The leader…" He trailed off, his jaw tightening. "They're inside the city, hiding in plain sight."

Kaelith's breath caught in her throat, her mind racing. "Who?" she asked, the word barely a whisper.

His lips parted as if he was about to say something, but then he stopped himself. The pause lingered, stretching out in the silence between them.

And then it happened.

A soft click—the unmistakable sound of a hidden door opening.

Kaelith's eyes shot to the source of the sound. She spun around, her heart racing, and saw a shadow moving at the edge of the room. The flicker of movement was too fast to identify, but it was enough to set her instincts on edge.

In one fluid motion, she turned back to face Rhyzor, only to find him no longer standing where he had been. The space he occupied was now empty. He had vanished.

Her pulse thundered in her ears.

Something was wrong.

Kaelith reached for the dagger at her waist, her fingers brushing the hilt, her grip tightening.

The door to the chambers closed softly, and the sound of footsteps faded into the night.

She stood there, frozen, every muscle tense.

Was he a traitor? Had he been working against her all along? Was this his way of setting her up?

Had he manipulated her from the very beginning?

Her heart pounded in her chest, the weight of the decisions she had made suddenly crashing down on her like a thousand tons of stone. She had trusted him. She had given him power, a position at her side. She had chosen him over the kingdom's law, over the advice of her council.

And now, everything felt like it was unraveling.

The moonlight outside the window caught something—a faint glint of metal—and Kaelith's eyes darted toward it. Her breath hitched as she saw a small, polished dagger lying on the floor near the edge of the room. It was hers.

Her own dagger.

And it had been placed carefully—purposefully—on the floor near the hidden door.

Her mind raced as she picked it up, her fingers tracing the intricate designs etched into the blade.

This was no accident.

This was a message.

She could feel the adrenaline coursing through her veins as she crossed the room to the small hidden door. There was only one person who could have left that dagger there.

The truth hit her like a tidal wave.

Rhyzor had betrayed her.

The dagger had been a warning—a sign that she was not in control. That he was pulling the strings now.

With shaking hands, Kaelith moved toward the door, the hairs on the back of her neck standing up. She pushed the door open with a quiet creak, her heart thudding in her chest.

The passage beyond was dark, the walls narrow and oppressive. She took a deep breath and stepped into the darkness. Her instincts were sharp, every step calculated as she moved through the labyrinth of corridors beneath the palace.

At the end of the passage, the dim light of the torch flickered, and she saw him.

Rhyzor.

He was standing there, his back to her, his posture relaxed as if nothing had changed.

But it had. Everything had changed.

"I should have known," she said, her voice low, tight with anger. "You've been playing me from the start."

Rhyzor turned slowly, and for a moment, his golden eyes gleamed with something—something almost like regret. But it was gone in an instant, replaced by the cold, calculating expression she had come to know so well.

"You always did see through me," he said, his voice softer now, but no less dangerous. "But I never needed you to see me. I needed you to trust me."

The words hit her harder than any weapon.

"You used me," Kaelith said, the words thick with disbelief. "You used my throne, my people, my trust."

Rhyzor stepped closer, his eyes locked on hers. "And what did you expect? You thought you could give me power, let me live, and not expect me to use it for my own purposes?"

"You were never loyal," she whispered.

"I was never meant to be loyal," he answered simply.

The air between them crackled with tension, every word another strike, every movement another piece of the puzzle falling into place.

Kaelith raised her dagger, her hand steady despite the storm of emotions tearing through her. "You will pay for this."

Rhyzor's gaze flickered down to the blade, then back to her face. "Go ahead. Kill me."

But Kaelith hesitated, her grip on the dagger tightening as the reality of the situation set in.

Killing him would be the easy choice, the swift solution. But something inside her—something deeper than the rage or the betrayal—held her back.

"You will regret this," she said, her voice colder than the dungeon walls.

Rhyzor's smile was cold and empty. "I already do."

With that, he turned away, his figure swallowed by the shadows of the passage.

And Kaelith was left alone, the dagger still gripped tightly in her hand, the weight of his betrayal sinking deep into her chest like a poison.

Eight

To Trust a Foe

The heavy clouds hung like a shroud over the city of Veyrith, an oppressive gray that matched the dark thoughts swirling in Kaelith's mind. The palace courtyard lay silent as she walked through it, her boots clicking sharply on the cobblestone, the sound echoing against the stone walls. She had not slept. Could not sleep. Every shadow seemed to whisper of betrayal.

The dagger Rhyzor had left behind still rested on her bedside table, its cold steel a constant reminder of the decision that had been made. She had given him a chance. A chance he had used against her. And now she had to face the consequences of her trust.

Her thoughts were interrupted by a voice that cut through the fog of her mind.

"Your Majesty."

Kaelith turned to find General Varek standing in the shadow of the palace archway. His tall form was cloaked in shadows, his usual composure fractured only by the tightness around his jaw.

"We need to talk," he said, his voice low, controlled.

She nodded, her mind racing. "Where?"

"Inside. The council awaits."

Her stomach churned. The council. The men who had once pledged loyalty to her mother. The men who had witnessed her rise to power, and now—she feared—some of them may be the ones who sought to undermine her rule.

Varek led the way back through the marble halls, his pace quick, yet measured. He did not glance back, and Kaelith followed without a word. Her thoughts drifted to the image of Rhyzor, standing in the shadows, his smile cold and calculating. His betrayal had stung like a blade driven through her chest, but there was more to it—something deeper that gnawed at her. She had trusted him. And now, she wondered if that trust was the last mistake she would make.

As they entered the council chamber, Kaelith felt the weight of all the eyes that turned toward her. The long table was surrounded by nobles and generals, their faces a mixture of concern, skepticism, and something else she could not place. Lord Jeren's gaze lingered on her, filled with unspoken questions.

"Your Majesty," he said, his tone polite, but his eyes narrowed in scrutiny. "We are awaiting your decisions."

Kaelith's gaze shifted across the room. Her council was divided—half of them had long supported her rule, while the others had not forgotten her mother's reign. She knew, deep down, that the loyalty of the latter group was fragile at best.

"I have not yet made a decision," Kaelith replied, her voice firm, though her heart raced with a mix of dread and anticipation.

Varek took a step forward, his hand resting on the back of a chair. "The rebellion is growing stronger. We've received word of movements in the southern districts. This is no longer just a whisper among the people—it is an organized effort."

Kaelith nodded, her fingers tightening around the armrest. "And where does Rhyzor stand in all of this?"

Varek's jaw tightened, but he did not hesitate. "He is the key to everything. We know his loyalty is uncertain, but his connection to the rebels—"

"—Is undeniable," Kaelith finished. She turned toward the council. "I have made a decision. I will meet with Rhyzor."

A ripple of murmurs passed through the room, a wave of disbelief washing over the faces around her. Lord Jeren's eyes widened, his voice rising.

"Your Majesty, surely you are not considering this. He is a traitor. A threat to the throne. You cannot trust him."

"I am aware of his betrayal," Kaelith replied coldly. "But he knows something we do not. And if there is even the slightest chance that he can be turned, I must take it."

A heavy silence settled over the room, the weight of her words hanging in the air like a storm ready to break. General Varek's gaze softened, and he gave a barely perceptible nod, as though understanding the delicate balance Kaelith was attempting to strike.

"You will meet with him alone?" Lord Cailan asked, his voice laced with skepticism.

Kaelith did not falter. "Yes."

She turned on her heel, leaving the council chamber without another word. Behind her, the low murmur of disagreement followed, but she refused to let it deter her. This was her decision, and no one would dictate her course now—not even the men who had sworn to serve her.

The hallway was cold as she made her way toward the dungeons. Each step felt heavier than the last. Rhyzor's betrayal was still fresh in her mind, but something inside her—something deeper—told her this meeting was necessary. She would not be swayed by the doubts of others. Not this time.

The dungeon doors loomed ahead, the guards standing at attention as she approached. Her hand hovered over the iron handle, and for a moment, she hesitated.

What if he betrayed her again? What if he used this moment to strike the final blow to her rule?

She exhaled slowly and opened the door. The air inside was thick, damp, and the scent of stale stone filled her lungs. At the far end of the cell, Rhyzor stood, his back to her, his shoulders rigid. The moment she entered, his head tilted slightly, as though sensing her presence.

"You came," he said quietly, without turning to face her.

"I said I would," Kaelith replied, her voice steady despite the storm of emotions raging inside her.

For a moment, neither of them spoke. The silence was heavy, suffocating.

Then, Rhyzor turned, his golden eyes flashing in the dim light. "What do you want, Kaelith?"

She met his gaze, her mind racing, her heart caught between anger and something else—something far more dangerous.

"You know what I want," she said softly. "The truth."

Rhyzor's smirk appeared, slow and knowing. "And what makes you think I will give it to you?"

"Because you need me." The words felt sharp as a blade. "I know you, Rhyzor. You don't want to die in a dungeon, and you don't want to see your people destroyed."

For the briefest moment, she saw a flicker of something in his eyes—something like doubt. But it was gone as quickly as it had appeared.

"Perhaps," he said, his voice low. "But I will not fight for your throne, Kaelith. Not for you."

Her breath caught in her throat, but she forced herself to hold his gaze. "You don't have a choice."

His gaze softened just a fraction, and Kaelith knew, in that moment, that the battle was not over. She had crossed a line. The tension between them was thick, but underneath it, there was an unspoken understanding. They both knew the risks of this meeting—of what could happen if either of them faltered.

"You want me to betray my own people," he said, his voice low, dangerous. "To become your pawn."

"I want you to help me," she replied. "And in return, I will give you the power you've always sought."

For a long moment, they simply stood there, the distance between them more than physical. Then, finally, Rhyzor's voice broke the silence again.

"I don't believe you, Kaelith."

Her heart clenched, but she forced herself to remain composed. "Believe what you will. But if we don't end this rebellion now, we will both lose everything."

Rhyzor's gaze never wavered. "And if I refuse?"

Kaelith felt the weight of the decision press down on her. She had already made too many mistakes—she would not let this one be the last.

"You will do what is necessary," she said. "For both our sakes."

He stepped closer, his expression unreadable. "And if I cannot trust you?"

She met his gaze, her own steely resolve firming. "Then you will regret it."

Rhyzor looked at her for a long moment, the tension hanging between them like a blade waiting to fall. Finally, he gave a small nod.

"I will help you," he said, his voice cold, but there was a flicker of something beneath it. "But remember this, Kaelith—nothing is ever as it seems. And you might just find out that the price for my loyalty is higher than you're willing to pay."

Her heart skipped a beat, but she nodded.

"Then let's begin."

Nine

A Queen's Secret Desire

The moonlight poured in through the tall windows of Kaelith's chamber, casting long, pale shadows across the floor. The city of Veyrith lay beneath a blanket of silence, the faintest echo of distant activity whispering through the streets. But here, in the heart of the palace, all was still. It was as if time itself had frozen, caught between the weight of the decisions Kaelith had made and the ones yet to come.

Her fingers traced the edges of the map spread out before her on the table. The rebellion was spreading faster than she had anticipated, its tendrils creeping into the southern districts, into the hearts of the very people she had sworn to protect. The names of the leaders still eluded her, and every moment without answers gnawed at her like a constant ache.

She had given Rhyzor a chance.

And now, she could feel the consequences of that decision pressing down on her. The coldness of betrayal still lingered in the air, but it was accompanied by something else—something she couldn't name.

Something dangerous.

Kaelith leaned back in her chair, exhaling sharply. Her thoughts were a tangled mess, her mind racing with what had transpired in the dungeon, with the quiet agreement she had struck with Rhyzor. He had agreed to help her, but his words—his promise to make her regret it—haunted her. His intentions, his motives, were unclear. But what was clearer than anything was that the tenuous line between them was one wrong move away from snapping entirely.

There was no room for weakness, no room for indecision.

But then there was the matter of Rhyzor himself.

Kaelith's heart thudded in her chest as she thought of the look in his eyes the last time they had spoken. The way he had stood so close, the raw intensity between them, almost palpable. She had made her choice to trust him, but in that moment, something else stirred beneath her resolve.

Something she could no longer ignore.

Her breath caught as she remembered the way his hand had brushed against hers during their brief moments together—when their eyes had locked, and there had been no walls between them. For a moment, she had felt something shift, something more than a simple alliance of convenience.

But she could not afford to let such thoughts cloud her judgment. She was a queen. She had a duty to her people, to her kingdom, and nothing—nothing—could stand in the way of that. Not even Rhyzor.

A knock at the door broke her thoughts, the sound cutting through the stillness of the room.

"Enter."

The door creaked open, and Varek stepped inside, his expression serious.

"My queen," he began, his voice low, almost apologetic. "The council wishes to meet with you. They demand answers."

Kaelith nodded, standing up from the table and smoothing her gown. "I'll be there shortly."

Varek hesitated for a moment, then spoke again, his tone a touch hesitant. "There is also… another matter, my queen."

Kaelith looked at him, her brow furrowing slightly. "What is it?"

Varek glanced toward the door, as if ensuring they were alone, before stepping closer. "It concerns Rhyzor. Some of the guards have spoken of seeing him outside his quarters tonight. He was not where he was supposed to be."

Kaelith's pulse quickened, but she masked it with a cold gaze. "What do you mean, not where he was supposed to be?"

Varek's lips pressed together in a thin line. "Some say they saw him near the northern gates, conversing with figures cloaked in shadow. I cannot say for certain, but it's... troubling."

Kaelith's heart sank. "You believe he's involved with the rebels?"

Varek didn't reply immediately, but the weight of his silence was enough to make Kaelith's stomach tighten. She had trusted him. She had given him a chance. And now, just as quickly as the walls between them had crumbled, they seemed to be rising again.

"He is dangerous," Varek said softly, almost as if speaking to himself. "We cannot ignore this."

Kaelith swallowed hard, her fingers curling into fists. "Thank you, Varek. I'll handle it from here."

The general gave a stiff bow, but his eyes lingered on her for a moment, as though uncertain of her next move. With one final glance, he turned and left, closing the door behind him with a soft click.

Kaelith stood in the middle of the room, her mind a whirlwind of conflicting emotions. She had suspected this moment would come. She had feared it, even. Rhyzor's loyalty was a fragile thing—born of necessity, not trust. And now, his shadow seemed to stretch even further, threatening to engulf everything she had worked for.

Her thoughts turned to him again—the way he had looked at her when they stood in the dungeon together. The fire in his eyes had been unmistakable. The power he wielded, the magnetism that had always drawn her in… she could feel it even now.

But she was a queen. She could not afford such distractions.

And yet, in the quietest moments, when she was alone with her thoughts, she couldn't help but wonder…

What if there was something more?

What if this was not just politics, not just power, but something deeper? Something she had long buried beneath the weight of her crown?

She pushed the thought aside, forcing herself to focus. This was not about her desires. This was about her kingdom. The future of Veyrith rested on her shoulders, and she would not falter.

But then why did she feel this ache in her chest every time Rhyzor's name crossed her mind?

Why did she find herself questioning whether she was truly just using him, or whether—deep down—she wanted more than just his help in vanquishing the rebellion?

The door opened again, and Kaelith turned quickly, her thoughts scattering like leaves in the wind.

The figure in the doorway was not Varek. It was Rhyzor.

He stood in the frame, the dim light casting shadows across his face, his golden eyes gleaming with an unreadable expression.

Kaelith's pulse quickened, but she refused to let him see it.

"Rhyzor," she said, her voice steady despite the wild beat of her heart. "What are you doing here?"

He stepped into the room, his gaze never leaving hers. "I had to see you," he said, his voice low, almost strained. "There are things I need to tell you. Things you need to know."

Kaelith's breath caught in her throat. "And why should I listen to you now? After everything?"

Rhyzor's jaw tightened, but he didn't flinch. "Because I don't want to be your enemy, Kaelith. I don't want to destroy you. I never did."

His words hung in the air like a confession, and Kaelith felt a strange mix of relief and suspicion wash over her.

"Then what is it you want from me?" she asked, her voice softer now, betraying none of the storm brewing inside her.

Rhyzor took a step closer, his presence overwhelming in the

stillness of the room. He didn't answer immediately. Instead, his eyes searched hers, as though trying to gauge the depth of her resolve.

"I want to help you," he said finally. "But there is a price. The price of your trust. The price of your… heart."

Kaelith froze. The words felt like a dagger, sharp and deliberate, sinking into her chest.

She opened her mouth to speak, but no words came.

Rhyzor moved closer still, his voice barely a whisper. "You don't have to fight this, Kaelith. We could—"

He didn't finish the sentence.

Instead, he reached for her, his hand brushing her cheek in the softest of touches, as though testing her response.

For a moment, everything else faded—the rebellion, the council, the kingdom. It was just the two of them in that moment, the air between them thick with something neither of them could deny.

And in that moment, Kaelith knew. She knew that this—whatever it was—was not just about power. Not just about the throne.

It was about something deeper. Something she had long buried beneath the weight of her crown.

But she was a queen.

And queens did not succumb to such desires. Not when everything else was on the line.

With a sharp breath, Kaelith stepped back, her voice cold and firm. "I cannot do this, Rhyzor."

For a moment, the flicker of hurt in his eyes was unmistakable. But then, it was gone, replaced by the familiar mask of control.

"I didn't expect you to," he said softly, his voice almost too quiet.

Kaelith met his gaze, her resolve hardening. "You will help me with the rebellion. You will do what I say. And nothing else."

Rhyzor nodded slowly, his golden eyes never leaving hers.

"Nothing else," he repeated.

And yet, as he turned to leave, Kaelith couldn't shake the feeling that something—something more—had just shifted between them. Something neither of them could ignore.

Ten

Flames of the Past

T he flicker of torchlight danced on the stone walls of the palace, casting long, stretching shadows that seemed to whisper secrets in the dark. Kaelith walked alone through the narrow corridors, her footsteps quiet but deliberate, the weight of the crown on her brow like a constant reminder of her duty. The soft clink of her armor as she moved was the only sound that accompanied her, echoing through the silence that had settled in the palace since her meeting with Rhyzor.

Tonight, she was restless—more so than usual. The lingering tension between her and the dragon prince had become unbearable. Each moment that passed without answers gnawed at her, the uncertainty weighing her down. She had made a choice, trusted him, and yet the doubt that had crept into her heart was still there. The suspicion. The fear that she had made a mistake.

But she couldn't ignore the pull of something deeper.

The truth was, she could no longer deny the connection between them. It wasn't just political. It wasn't just a matter of convenience or power. There was something in the way he looked at her, the way he spoke, that called to her in ways she couldn't fully understand.

As she passed through the shadowed halls, Kaelith's thoughts drifted back to the first time she had met Rhyzor—the first time their paths had crossed.

It had been years ago, during a time when she was still a girl, before the weight of the throne had settled on her shoulders. Back then, the world had been simpler—before the kingdom had crumbled, before the dragons had been slain, before the blood had been spilled.

She had been running through the forest, her feet barely touching the earth, when she had heard the sounds of movement—a rustle in the trees, a flicker of motion in the shadows. Her heart had raced, the thrill of the chase coursing through her veins. It was a game, a game she had played often, where the forest became her kingdom, and she was its ruler.

But this time, the game had changed.

She had rounded a corner, and there he was—standing still, as if waiting for her. His dark hair hung in wild strands around his face, and his golden eyes burned with an intensity that made her stop in her tracks.

He was unlike anyone she had ever seen.

"Lost, are we?" the boy had asked, his voice low, but with an edge to it that intrigued her.

Kaelith had bristled at the remark. She was no stranger to the forest; she had always been its master. But something about this boy unsettled her. He was tall, with the broad shoulders of someone who had known hard labor. His face was chiseled, almost regal, and there was a fire in his eyes—a fierceness that made her heart skip a beat.

"Who are you?" she demanded, her voice sharp.

He had smirked, the corners of his lips curling just slightly. "Does it matter?"

"Yes," she said, taking a step closer, her curiosity piqued despite herself. "It does."

The boy had paused for a moment, his eyes scanning her with a mix of disdain and amusement. "Rhyzor," he had finally said. "Prince of Rhaedros."

At that, Kaelith's breath had caught in her throat. She had heard of Rhaedros—the last kingdom of dragons. The kingdom her mother had crushed. The kingdom her family had destroyed.

"You're a dragon," she whispered.

Rhyzor's smirk deepened. "I was. But I'm still here, aren't I?"

Kaelith had narrowed her eyes, unsure of what to make of this strange, defiant boy standing before her. He was her enemy, the last heir to a people she had been taught to hate. And yet, something about him stirred something deep inside her—something she couldn't quite name.

He had stepped closer, his voice softer now. "The question is, princess, what will you do about it?"

Before she could respond, the sound of horses' hooves had echoed through the forest. Her heart had skipped, and in a flash, the moment had ended. She had turned and run, the memory of his gaze lingering long after he had disappeared into the shadows.

It had been years since that day, but the image of him—his burning eyes, his smile, the strange pull between them—had never left her. And now, standing in the corridors of the palace, those memories came rushing back, flooding her with a mixture of confusion and longing.

The past had a way of creeping up on her, twisting and pulling at her heartstrings when she least expected it. It was as if she couldn't escape it—no matter how hard she tried.

Kaelith reached the door to the royal garden and stepped outside, the cool night air brushing against her skin. The garden was a quiet oasis, filled with the scent of flowers and the soft rustling of leaves in the breeze. She walked slowly, taking in the peaceful stillness that surrounded her. It was a rare moment of calm in the storm that was her life.

And yet, she couldn't shake the feeling that something was about to change.

She stopped near a stone bench, her fingers grazing the edge as she gazed out over the darkened garden. The memories of her past seemed to collide with the present in that moment. The faces of her family—her mother's cold, calculating eyes, her father's stern gaze—flashed before her. And then, there was Rhyzor. The boy she had once known, the man he had become.

She thought she had buried the past. But the flames of it were rising again, threatening to consume everything she had built.

"You think you're safe," a voice said from behind her, low and calm, but with a dangerous edge.

Kaelith turned sharply, her heart racing, and there he was. Rhyzor. Standing in the shadows of the garden, his dark figure framed by the moonlight. His golden eyes gleamed, reflecting the faint light of the night.

For a long moment, neither of them spoke. The tension between them was thick, the air crackling with the unspoken history that bound them together.

"What do you want?" Kaelith asked, her voice cold, though she could feel the heat rising in her chest.

Rhyzor stepped forward, his expression unreadable. "To talk," he said, his voice soft but firm.

"Talk?" Kaelith echoed. "About what?"

"About the rebellion," Rhyzor said, his gaze fixed on her. "About the choices you're going to have to make. About the future of your kingdom."

Kaelith's pulse quickened. "What do you know about the future of my kingdom?"

Rhyzor's lips twitched, a ghost of a smile playing at the corners of his mouth. "More than you think."

Kaelith's eyes narrowed. "What are you really here for, Rhyzor?"

He was standing just a few paces away now, his presence overwhelming. The way he looked at her—his gaze burning with intensity—made her heart race, though she forced herself to remain composed.

"I'm here because you don't have a choice," he said softly. "You need me."

Kaelith shook her head, stepping back. "I don't need anyone."

Rhyzor's gaze softened, but the smirk never left his lips. "You've always been strong, Kaelith. But strength doesn't mean you don't need help."

His words struck her like a blow. He was right. She had always been strong, always been the one to carry the weight of her kingdom, her people, on her shoulders. But the truth was, she was tired. She was exhausted by the lies, the betrayals, the weight of the throne.

"I've never needed anyone," she said, her voice shaky now.

Rhyzor stepped closer, his eyes never leaving hers. "But you need me now. Whether you want to admit it or not."

The words hung in the air, and for the first time, Kaelith wasn't sure how to respond. The past had returned, not as a memory, but as a reality that was impossible to ignore.

And in that moment, standing there in the moonlit garden, with the distant echoes of rebellion rising in the background, Kaelith knew.

The flames of the past would burn everything down unless she chose to confront them.

But the question was: How?

Eleven

The War Council's Demand

The sound of Kaelith's boots echoed through the cold stone corridors of the war room, each step heavy with the weight of the decisions that awaited her. The palace was eerily quiet this morning, the usual hustle and bustle of the servants and nobles muted in the wake of the growing unrest. The rebellion had spread faster than anyone had anticipated. What had begun as whispers of dissent now threatened to boil over into full-scale rebellion. The walls of Veyrith felt like they were closing in on her, and the kingdom that had once seemed so secure now trembled at the edge of collapse.

As she approached the war council chamber, Kaelith's breath quickened, the air thick with tension. She had already spoken with her generals, but today, the real battle would begin. Today, she would face the men and women who had sworn allegiance

The War Council's Demand

to her—some of whom now questioned whether she deserved the throne. It was a fight of loyalty, and one she wasn't sure she could win.

The massive wooden doors swung open before her, and Kaelith stepped inside, her gaze immediately sweeping over the faces of the men and women seated at the long, polished table. There was no warmth in the room, no courtesy in the way they looked at her. Only suspicion, and beneath that, fear. Fear of what the future might hold.

Lord Jeren, the loudest of her critics, was the first to speak. "You're late, my queen," he said, his voice dripping with disdain.

Kaelith didn't flinch. She was used to his venom by now. "The situation is dire, Lord Jeren. I am not concerned with punctuality."

The council was silent for a moment as Kaelith took her seat at the head of the table, the weight of her position pressing down on her shoulders like a physical burden. The room was filled with the scent of burning incense, but it did little to mask the underlying tension in the air. The men and women in front of her were all seasoned strategists, battle-hardened, and had seen wars come and go. But they had never seen one like this—one that threatened not just their borders, but their very way of life.

"I trust you all know why we are gathered here today," Kaelith said, her voice steady but forceful. "The rebellion is no longer a threat in the distant shadows. It is here, in the heart of the kingdom, and we need to act before it spreads further."

Lord Cailan, ever the opportunist, leaned forward, his eyes gleaming with a mixture of fear and ambition. "My queen, we have waited long enough. The time for negotiations has passed. The rebels must be crushed, and they must be crushed quickly."

"And yet, we know nothing about who leads them," Kaelith countered. "We cannot fight an enemy we do not understand."

A murmur of agreement rippled through the council, but Lord Jeren scoffed. "Understand them? You think we need to understand the enemy, when all we need to do is wipe them out?" He slammed his fist onto the table, his face flushed with anger. "We've been too soft, Kaelith. Too hesitant. This is not a matter of diplomacy. It's war. And war demands a firm hand."

Kaelith's gaze hardened. "You speak as if war is some simple affair, Lord Jeren. It is not. Every battle we fight has consequences, and I will not sacrifice the lives of our people without understanding the full scope of what we face."

Varek, who had remained silent until now, leaned forward, his dark eyes sharp with focus. "We have spies. We have scouts. And yet, there is no clear leader of this rebellion. We know there are pockets of insurgents, but they remain fragmented. And we know one other thing—Rhyzor is involved."

The mention of his name sent a ripple through the room. All eyes turned to Kaelith, whose face remained an impassive mask.

"We cannot afford to ignore that, my queen," Varek continued. "He was once a prince of Rhaedros, and now he stands at the

The War Council's Demand

heart of the unrest. His connections run deep, and we must find a way to deal with him before we can move forward."

Kaelith's heart thudded painfully in her chest. The thought of Rhyzor—the boy she had once trusted, the man who had betrayed her—was a bitter pill to swallow. But she had known, deep down, that she could not avoid him forever.

She took a deep breath, steadying herself. "I have met with him."

A collective gasp echoed around the table, and Kaelith's gaze swept across the room. "You met with him?" Jeren demanded, his voice rising in disbelief.

"Yes," Kaelith replied, her tone unwavering. "And I will meet with him again if necessary."

The council erupted into chaos. "Are you mad, my queen?" Jeren shouted. "After everything he's done?"

"He is not just some common rebel," Kaelith said, her voice rising to silence the outbursts. "He is the last prince of a kingdom we destroyed. His anger is not without cause, and his betrayal was not born of malice, but of necessity. We must understand why he is doing this."

"I will not let our kingdom be torn apart because of your misplaced empathy," Lord Cailan snapped. "We must act now."

The tension in the room was palpable, the air thick with distrust and fear. Kaelith knew that she was losing them. Slowly but surely, they were slipping away from her.

She slammed her hand down on the table, the force of it shocking them into silence. "You will listen to me," she said, her voice steady and commanding. "Rhyzor will not be dismissed as a common enemy. His people have been erased from history. He has nothing left. And I will not let that be the legacy of this kingdom."

A heavy silence fell over the room. Kaelith's chest heaved with the weight of her words, but she could feel the weight of her crown, heavier than ever before. This was her kingdom, and it was slipping through her fingers.

"Then what do you propose we do?" Jeren asked, his voice quieter now, tinged with doubt.

Kaelith stood, pacing slowly across the room. She could feel their eyes on her, waiting for an answer, waiting for her to save them from this impending war. She knew what they wanted. They wanted a decision. A simple, clean solution to the mess they found themselves in.

But Kaelith knew there was no such thing.

"We will fight, yes," she said, her voice steady. "But we will fight with intelligence, not brute force. We will find the leader of this rebellion, and we will understand why they are rebelling. I will not sacrifice the lives of our people unless I know what we are fighting for."

The War Council's Demand

A murmur of disbelief passed through the room. "And what about Rhyzor?" Varek asked quietly. "What is your plan for him?"

Kaelith stopped in her tracks, her back to the council. She took a deep breath, feeling the weight of their expectations pressing down on her.

"I will confront him," she said softly. "And I will give him one final chance to prove his loyalty."

"Loyalty?" Jeren scoffed. "You are a fool, Kaelith. There is no loyalty left in him."

Kaelith turned to face him, her eyes hardening. "And yet, I am still the queen. You will follow my orders, or you will be dismissed."

The words hung in the air like a challenge, and for a moment, no one moved. But Kaelith's gaze never wavered.

"I will speak with Rhyzor," she continued. "And when I have what I need from him, we will strike. But we will not be the aggressors in this war. Not until we know our enemy."

A tense silence fell over the council, and Kaelith could see the hesitation in their eyes. They didn't trust her decisions. They didn't trust Rhyzor. And they certainly didn't trust the unknown path she was now forging. But they had no choice.

"You will carry out my orders," she repeated, her voice cold. "Or you will leave this council."

With those final words, Kaelith turned on her heel and strode toward the door. She didn't wait for their response. She didn't need it.

The war had begun. And with it, a new battle for the throne. One that would test her, not just as a ruler, but as a woman. A woman who had been forced to make impossible choices.

And as the doors closed behind her, Kaelith knew the hardest battle of all was just beginning.

Twelve

A Forbidden Alliance

The moon hung high in the sky, its pale light casting an eerie glow over the royal palace, where the stone walls seemed to pulse with the weight of history and betrayal. The city below was still, but within the chambers of the palace, the air was thick with tension, and it was here that Kaelith stood, alone, staring out into the night.

She had done the unthinkable. The very thought of what she had agreed to made her heart thud against her chest with a mixture of fear and anticipation. She had agreed to meet with Rhyzor again. She had agreed to seek an alliance with the last dragon prince, a man who was both her greatest enemy and, strangely, her only hope.

The rebellion was growing, its flames spreading across the southern districts like wildfire, and the only way to end it was to understand the enemy. To know who was behind it, to know the forces that were at play. Kaelith had been forced to acknowledge the truth she had tried to avoid for so long—Rhyzor was her only chance to control this war. But to align herself with him... it was a risk that could cost her everything.

Her breath came in shallow bursts as she turned from the window, her eyes briefly catching the reflection of her crown in the polished surface of a nearby mirror. The weight of the gold seemed to grow heavier every time she looked at it. She had always known the crown was a burden, but now, more than ever, it felt like a prison.

Her thoughts were interrupted by the quiet sound of footsteps approaching. She didn't need to turn around to know who it was.

"Your Majesty," General Varek's voice was low, his tone respectful but laced with concern.

Kaelith didn't look up as he entered the room, but she could feel his gaze on her. She could feel the tension in the air, the silent disapproval that hung between them. He had not agreed with her decision to meet with Rhyzor, but he had followed her orders without question. He was loyal, but even loyalty had its limits.

"General," Kaelith said, her voice calm but firm. "Is the council waiting for me?"

Varek hesitated for a moment before speaking again. "The

council is waiting, but I'm afraid there is more pressing news. The scouts report that the southern districts are in complete unrest. The rebellion has taken control of several villages, and we are losing ground. If we don't act quickly, we could lose the entire region."

She turned to face him, her eyes steely. "And you believe an alliance with Rhyzor will stop that?"

Varek didn't answer immediately. Instead, he stepped closer, his eyes searching hers. "My queen," he said softly, "this… this is dangerous. He is the son of your enemy. Do you truly believe he can be trusted?"

Kaelith's jaw clenched, her fingers tightening into fists. "I have no choice. The rebellion grows stronger by the hour, and the council… they want war. They want to strike first, burn the rebels to the ground. But that will not solve anything. It will only drive more people to join their cause."

Varek sighed, his shoulders slumping slightly. "I understand your reasoning, but I fear that your trust in him—"

"Is not about trust," she cut him off, her voice rising just slightly. "It is about survival. If I don't take this risk, we may lose the kingdom altogether."

There was a long silence between them, the weight of her words hanging in the air. Finally, Varek nodded, though his expression remained troubled.

"Very well," he said. "But I must warn you, my queen, this alliance—should it even be possible—will come at a price. He will not help us out of the goodness of his heart. There is something he wants, something we have not yet seen."

Kaelith's gaze hardened. "I am not blind to that, General. But we must take what we can get, even if it means playing a dangerous game."

Varek gave a curt nod. "As you wish, my queen."

Without another word, he turned and left the room, leaving Kaelith alone with her thoughts once more. She stood still for a moment, the weight of her decision pressing down on her like a heavy fog. Every instinct screamed at her to back away, to refuse the dangerous path she was about to take. But the thought of the rebellion spreading unchecked, of her kingdom crumbling beneath the weight of its own discord, was enough to silence those instincts.

Tonight, she would meet with Rhyzor. The forbidden alliance would begin.

The door to her chambers opened once again, and a servant stepped inside, bowing low.

"My queen," the servant said. "The meeting has been arranged. Prince Rhyzor is waiting for you in the northern courtyard."

Kaelith's heart skipped a beat. She gave a silent nod, her breath catching in her throat. It was time.

A Forbidden Alliance

She moved swiftly, her cloak trailing behind her as she made her way to the courtyard. The hallways seemed endless, the cold stone walls closing in on her as she passed through them. Every footstep felt like it was leading her closer to an unknown fate.

As she approached the courtyard, she could see the flicker of torchlight in the distance, and in the center of the open space stood Rhyzor. His dark form was outlined against the night sky, the wind ruffling his black hair. His golden eyes gleamed in the dim light as he turned toward her, and for a moment, their gazes locked.

Kaelith felt the familiar pull between them, the same magnetism that had once drawn her to him as a girl. But now, it was different. There was no innocence left between them, no childhood memories to soften the edges. What had once been a flicker of something tender was now a dangerous, smoldering fire.

Rhyzor smiled, but it was the kind of smile that didn't quite reach his eyes.

"My queen," he said softly, his voice as smooth and dangerous as ever. "I see you've come."

Kaelith squared her shoulders, stepping into the courtyard with a steady, unwavering step. "I've come because I have no choice, Rhyzor."

He chuckled, a dark, knowing sound that seemed to echo in

the stillness of the night. "None of us ever do, do we?"

Kaelith stopped a few paces away from him, her eyes narrowing slightly. "I trust you understand the gravity of what we are about to do. The rebellion is on the edge of consuming everything. If we do not act swiftly, it will be too late."

Rhyzor's gaze shifted toward the palace, the city beyond it, his expression unreadable. "You think an alliance with me will save you?"

Kaelith met his gaze with the full force of her determination. "I think it's the only chance we have. You may not want to fight for my kingdom, but you know as well as I do that if this rebellion succeeds, there will be nothing left for either of us."

His eyes flickered with something that almost looked like amusement. "You think too highly of me, Kaelith. But I suppose, in this moment, you have no choice but to trust me."

"I trust no one," she said flatly. "But I have no other option."

Rhyzor stepped closer, his movements fluid and deliberate. "Then we are in agreement, aren't we? You need me, and I… need you."

Kaelith's heart thudded heavily in her chest, but she refused to let the emotions of the moment overwhelm her. "What is it that you want in return, Rhyzor?"

He met her gaze, his golden eyes piercing. "I want my people back. The power that was stolen from me. You can help me regain it—or I will leave you to deal with this rebellion alone."

A dangerous silence hung between them, the weight of his words sinking into Kaelith's chest. For a moment, she considered walking away, rejecting this dangerous offer. But she knew it would be a lie. Without his help, her kingdom would be lost, and all that remained would be ashes.

"You will get what you want," Kaelith said, her voice steady but filled with the steel of a queen who had seen the price of survival. "But if you betray me, if you betray my people, I will not hesitate to see you destroyed."

Rhyzor's smirk deepened. "I don't believe you, Kaelith. But I do believe that you're a queen who will do whatever it takes to save her kingdom."

Kaelith stepped back, her resolve firming. "Then we have an agreement. But remember, Rhyzor, this is a delicate game. One wrong move, and we both lose."

His gaze softened for a moment, almost imperceptibly. "I'm not in the business of losing."

As he turned to walk away, Kaelith stood motionless, her heart still racing in her chest. The forbidden alliance had begun. And with it, a new chapter in the battle for her kingdom, one that would test her strength, her resolve, and everything she had ever believed in.

The stakes had never been higher.

Thirteen

The Shadowed Oath

The air in the war council chamber was stifling, the heavy scent of incense mingling with the tension that had settled over the room. Kaelith sat at the head of the long table, her fingers drumming absentmindedly against the polished wood, her thoughts far from the proceedings. The rebellion had claimed the southern districts, and the fires of revolt spread like a disease, quickly taking root in the hearts of the people. The kingdom was on the brink of collapse, and yet, she could not bring herself to focus on anything but the oath she had just sworn—an oath to Rhyzor, a forbidden alliance forged in the shadows.

The men around the table spoke, their voices rising and falling with the rhythm of urgency, but Kaelith's mind was elsewhere. The last dragon prince. Her enemy, her ally. She had given him everything, trusting him with the future of her kingdom, even as the gnawing voice of doubt echoed in her mind. What if she had made a mistake? What if Rhyzor's motives were far more dangerous than even she could comprehend?

"My queen?"

The voice of General Varek cut through her reverie, and Kaelith snapped back to the present. She met his gaze, finding the same steely resolve she had always seen in his eyes. He had been with her through countless battles, yet even he seemed unnerved by the situation now.

"What is it, General?" she asked, her voice firm, though the storm inside her raged on.

"We have word from the scouts," Varek said, his tone grim. "The southern rebels have rallied behind a leader—a man they are calling the Flamebringer. They are no longer disorganized. They are a force, and they are headed straight for the capital."

Kaelith's heart skipped a beat. The name Flamebringer echoed in her mind like a warning. It was a title forged in fire, in death, and in blood. She had known this moment was coming—the day when the rebellion would take shape under a leader who could unify the fractured factions. But she had hoped, prayed, that the rebels would remain disjointed. That they would fall apart under the weight of their own disorganization. She had been wrong.

"Do we know anything about this Flamebringer?" Kaelith asked, her voice steady, though her mind raced.

The Shadowed Oath

"Only rumors, my queen," Varek replied, his expression grim. "They say he's ruthless—uncompromising. His forces are not like the rebels we've seen so far. They're trained, they're armed, and they're committed to the cause." He paused. "And they are marching on the capital."

The weight of the words hung in the air, and Kaelith's stomach twisted. The rebellion had always been an abstract threat, a vague enemy. But now, it was real. It had a face, a leader, and a purpose. The capital would be their next target, and if they succeeded—if this Flamebringer managed to breach the walls—there would be nothing left of Veyrith but ashes and ruin.

She pushed the rising panic aside, focusing on the task at hand. "We need to prepare the defenses," she said, her voice commanding. "We cannot afford to underestimate them."

Her words were met with murmurs of agreement, and the council members began to speak among themselves, organizing plans, discussing logistics. But even as they spoke, Kaelith's thoughts drifted once again to the forbidden oath she had made. The one she had sworn to Rhyzor. The price of the alliance. The price of her soul.

The night was cold when Kaelith made her way to the northern courtyard, where Rhyzor awaited her. The winds howled through the open spaces of the palace, carrying with them the scent of rain and earth. The moon hung low in the sky, casting its pale light across the stone, but it did little to quell the storm that raged inside her.

She had agreed to meet with him, to discuss the next steps in their alliance, but something about the night felt wrong. Every step she took felt heavier than the last, and the weight of her decisions threatened to swallow her whole. What had she truly promised Rhyzor? What had she given him that she could never take back?

When she reached the courtyard, Rhyzor was standing by the fountain, his back to her. He didn't turn as she approached, his posture relaxed, his face unreadable. The soft murmur of the water was the only sound that filled the air, and for a moment, Kaelith wondered if the gods were watching—if they, too, saw the path she was about to walk.

"Rhyzor," she said, her voice firm, though the doubt lingered.

He turned slowly, his golden eyes meeting hers. There was something in them—something that unsettled her. It wasn't just the cold determination she had seen before. No, there was something else. A shadow. A darkness.

"My queen," he said, his voice as smooth as ever, but with a slight edge. "I see you've come."

"I've come to talk," Kaelith replied, her gaze never leaving his. "We need to discuss our next move."

Rhyzor stepped closer, his movements slow and deliberate. "We've already discussed our next move, Kaelith. The rebellion is here. It's real. And you've given me the power to lead it."

She stiffened, a flash of irritation sparking inside her. "This is not just about you, Rhyzor. This is about Veyrith. This is about saving the kingdom from the flames of war."

"And what if I told you," Rhyzor said, his voice low, almost a whisper, "that the flames were never meant to be extinguished? What if I told you that I have waited for this moment for far longer than you could ever understand?"

Kaelith's heart skipped a beat. There was something in his words, something in the way he said them, that sent a chill down her spine. She had always known that Rhyzor had his own ambitions, his own desires. But now, those desires seemed to twist around her like a coil, tightening with every word he spoke.

"You promised me loyalty," she said, her voice steady, though her breath quickened. "You swore that you would help me end the rebellion. That you would help me save my kingdom."

"And I will," Rhyzor replied, his smile widening just slightly. "But you must understand something, Kaelith. My loyalty is not to the kingdom. It never was. My loyalty is to something greater."

Kaelith's breath caught in her throat, and for the first time, she saw the true extent of Rhyzor's ambition. She had known he was dangerous, but this—this was something else entirely. She had walked into this alliance thinking she could control him, thinking she could use his knowledge and his power to defeat the rebellion. But now, she wondered if she had been blind all along.

"What is it you want, Rhyzor?" she asked, her voice barely a whisper.

He stepped closer still, his eyes never leaving hers. "I want what was taken from me. What was stolen from my people. I want vengeance. And I will not rest until it is mine."

A chill ran through Kaelith. She knew, in that moment, that she had made a grave mistake. Rhyzor was not her ally. He had never been. He had always been playing a different game—one she hadn't fully understood.

"You think this is just about power," Kaelith said, her voice cold. "You think that if you burn everything to the ground, you'll rebuild it in your image. But you're wrong, Rhyzor. The kingdom is not yours to claim. The people are not yours to control."

Rhyzor's gaze softened, but there was something almost pitying in it. "And you think I want control, Kaelith? You think I want to be a king? I've already told you—I want vengeance. I want to see everything that has been taken from me returned to its rightful place. And if that means tearing down your kingdom, so be it."

The words cut through her like a blade, and for a moment, Kaelith didn't know how to respond. Her kingdom, her people, everything she had fought for—Rhyzor was willing to destroy it all to avenge his own loss. And she had given him the means to do it.

"I gave you power," Kaelith said through gritted teeth. "And you will use that power to help me. Not to destroy everything I've worked for."

Rhyzor's eyes narrowed, the intensity of his gaze growing sharper. "You think you control me, Kaelith? You think you can use me as a pawn in your game? You made a promise, and I've kept mine. But I never promised you peace. I promised you fire."

The air around them seemed to thicken, as though the very atmosphere was charged with the energy of their confrontation. Kaelith felt a sharp pang of fear twist in her chest, but she pushed it down. She had to remain strong.

"You swore an oath to me," she said, her voice low and dangerous. "And I expect you to keep it. Or I will make sure you regret ever crossing me."

Rhyzor's smile returned, though it was colder now. "An oath, Kaelith, is a fragile thing. And promises made in the shadow of power are often broken."

He turned and began to walk away, his cloak billowing behind him, the darkness of the night swallowing him whole.

Kaelith stood frozen, the weight of his words pressing down

on her. The fire that Rhyzor promised was not a fire she could control. And with every passing moment, she wondered if she had just set her kingdom alight.

The shadows had claimed their oath. And now, it was time to see if she could survive the flames.

Fourteen

A Kingdom Divided

The sun had barely risen over Veyrith, its pale light struggling to pierce the thick clouds that had settled over the city. The air felt heavy, as though it were holding its breath, waiting for something—a storm, a change, a reckoning. The streets of the capital were quieter than usual, the once-bustling marketplaces now eerily empty, the silence broken only by the distant sound of clashing swords and the muffled cries of those who dared to speak out against the growing unrest.

Kaelith stood on the balcony of her chamber, her hands gripping the cold stone railing as she looked down at the city below. Her kingdom. Her people.

And yet, in her heart, she felt the painful truth settling in: it was no longer the kingdom she had known. It was a kingdom divided.

The rebellion had spread like wildfire, igniting every corner of the land. The southern districts were lost to the insurgents, their flames rising higher with each passing day. The northern borders were under constant threat, with reports of skirmishes and ambushes coming in from every direction. Her kingdom, once strong and united, was now fractured. And every step she took to mend it only seemed to drive it further apart.

The decision to meet with Rhyzor had seemed like the only choice at the time. She had promised him an alliance, a pact forged in the shadows, a way to end the chaos. But now, with every passing moment, the weight of that decision grew heavier. Rhyzor had played his part, but it had become clear to her that he had never truly been an ally. His promises of vengeance, his thirst for power—it was all leading her down a path she had no intention of following. But how could she undo it? How could she extricate herself from the dangerous game she had willingly entered?

"Your Majesty."

Kaelith turned to see General Varek standing at the door of her chamber, his face grim, his eyes hard with the weight of the reports he had been gathering.

"My queen," he repeated, bowing low but not waiting for her response before stepping into the room.

"What is it, General?" Kaelith asked, her voice betraying none of the anxiety that knotted her insides.

Varek's expression softened for a moment, but he was quick to mask it with his usual stoicism. "The situation is worsening, my queen. We have reports of rebel forces moving closer to the capital. The southern districts are nearly lost, and the Flamebringer has amassed a significant force. It seems the rebellion has grown stronger, and we are not prepared to fight it head-on."

Kaelith felt her breath hitch, but she didn't allow herself to falter. She couldn't. Not now. Not when so many lives depended on her.

"And the council?" she asked, her voice low.

Varek's face tightened. "The council demands immediate action. They want to strike before the rebellion spreads further. They want to send a force to meet the rebels at the northern gate."

"And what do you advise, General?"

Varek hesitated, as though weighing his words carefully. "The council wants war, my queen. They are blind to the consequences of an all-out battle. But they have no stomach for negotiation, and no faith that we can resolve this without bloodshed."

Kaelith stood still, the weight of his words settling over her. She knew the council. She knew how they operated. They were loyal only to the throne, to the idea of power and control. And they feared the rebellion. Fear was the root of every decision they made.

"I will not bow to their demands," Kaelith said firmly, her voice cutting through the tension in the room. "We will not throw away lives for a war we don't yet understand. We will find a way to end this without sacrificing our future."

Varek's eyes searched hers for a moment, his face betraying a flicker of uncertainty. "And if the rebellion is not so easily stopped?"

"We will stop it together," Kaelith replied, her voice unwavering. "But we will not destroy Veyrith in the process."

Varek gave a short nod, but the concern in his eyes remained. Kaelith could see that he, too, was beginning to wonder whether her decisions were leading them down the right path. The rebellion had grown beyond anything they had prepared for, and the longer she delayed action, the more dangerous it became.

"I'll make sure the council is aware of your decision," Varek said, his voice heavy with unspoken words. "But be prepared for resistance. They are not known for their patience."

Kaelith nodded, her mind already working, already calculating the next steps. "I will go to the council. But I need to meet with Rhyzor first. There are things I need to know."

Varek's eyes flashed with concern. "My queen, I urge you not to—"

"I will meet with him, General," Kaelith said firmly, cutting him off. "We need to understand who is leading this rebellion, and Rhyzor is the key."

Varek opened his mouth to argue, but then he seemed to think better of it. He bowed, his gaze lingering on her for a moment before he turned and left the room.

Kaelith stood alone in the silence, the weight of the decision pressing down on her once more. The city was on the verge of collapse, the rebellion threatening to tear it apart. The council was impatient, and her kingdom was divided. In one corner, the fire of revolt burned brighter with every passing hour, and in the other, the cold weight of the throne demanded she make decisions that could reshape the future of Veyrith.

And she was stuck in the middle.

The night was cold when Kaelith made her way to the northern courtyard once more. The air was thick with the scent of rain, and the distant sound of thunder rumbled like a warning in the distance. She felt the tension in her muscles, the unease swirling in her chest. The promise she had made to Rhyzor still haunted her, but there was no turning back. She needed him now—whether she wanted to or not.

As she entered the courtyard, she saw him standing by the edge of the fountain again, his dark figure outlined against the storm-darkened sky. Rhyzor turned as she approached, his golden eyes gleaming with something unreadable.

"You came," he said, his voice low and smooth, the slight edge of something dangerous lingering in his words.

Kaelith stopped a few paces away from him, her heart pounding in her chest. "We need to talk," she said, her voice steady, though her mind raced with a thousand questions. "This rebellion is no longer a shadow. It is a force, and we need to understand who is leading it."

Rhyzor stepped closer, his eyes never leaving hers. "I told you before, Kaelith. I can help you. But nothing comes for free."

Kaelith's jaw tightened. "I'm not here for more of your riddles. I need answers."

He smiled, but it was a dangerous, predatory smile. "The Flamebringer—you've heard of him, haven't you?"

Kaelith's breath caught in her throat. The name had been whispered in the streets, but the full weight of it had never truly registered until now. The Flamebringer. It sounded like a title forged in blood, in fire, in vengeance. It was the name of a leader—a man who had united the fractured rebels, who had brought them together under one banner. And if that man truly existed, he was the one person who could bring down Veyrith.

"Yes," Kaelith said, her voice steady. "I've heard the rumors. I need to know more."

Rhyzor's smile faded slightly, his expression growing more serious. "The Flamebringer is not just a man, Kaelith. He is the embodiment of everything that has been lost. He is the last of my people—what remains of the dragon blood. He has a claim to what you have taken from us."

Kaelith felt her heart skip a beat. "You are not saying…?"

Rhyzor's eyes flickered with something dark. "I'm saying that he is the one who will burn everything to the ground unless we stop him."

Kaelith's thoughts swirled in a whirlwind of confusion and revelation. The leader of the rebellion—the one who had managed to unite the scattered insurgents—was connected to Rhyzor. And what's more, he carried with him the weight of the dragon blood, the same bloodline Rhyzor had inherited. The implications were staggering.

"If the Flamebringer is as dangerous as you say," Kaelith said, her voice tight, "then we have no time to waste."

Rhyzor nodded. "Indeed. But be careful, Kaelith. The path you're walking with me—it's a path that will lead you into the flames."

The air between them seemed to thicken, the tension rising like the storm in the distance. Kaelith had always known that she was walking a dangerous path. But now, as Rhyzor's words echoed in her mind, she realized the full extent of the danger she was in. The rebellion was no longer just a political struggle. It was a war for survival. A war that could tear her kingdom apart.

And at the heart of it all, stood Rhyzor—her forbidden ally.

A man who had the power to either save her kingdom or destroy it.

The question was no longer if they would survive. The question was: Who would survive the flames?

Fifteen

Beneath Dragon Wings

The sky was heavy with the promise of a storm, the clouds rolling across the horizon like a dark tide threatening to consume everything in its path. The wind had picked up, howling through the trees and rattling the windows of the palace. Kaelith stood on the edge of the balcony, her hands gripping the cold stone railing as she stared out into the gathering storm.

It felt as though the world was holding its breath, waiting for something—waiting for the storm to break. And in a way, it was. Beneath the storm clouds, beneath the winds and the crashing thunder, her kingdom was poised on the brink of destruction. The rebellion had grown stronger with each passing day. The Flamebringer was a force unlike any Kaelith had ever faced, and the council's demands for immediate action were growing louder.

Yet, in the shadows of it all, there was Rhyzor.

The man she had once trusted, the man she had once known, was now the key to saving her kingdom—or destroying it completely. She had sworn an oath to him. A dangerous oath that tied her fate to his, and as the winds howled around her, Kaelith couldn't shake the sense that the storm was coming for both of them. The question now wasn't whether the rebellion would be defeated. It was whether they would survive the war they had inadvertently started.

She heard the soft creak of the door behind her and turned, her pulse quickening despite herself. Rhyzor stood in the doorway, his tall form framed by the flickering light of the torches in the hall. The tension between them had been building for days, each moment they shared weighted with the unspoken truth that neither of them could escape: their alliance had bound them together in ways neither could control.

"You're here," Kaelith said, her voice steady, though her heart hammered in her chest.

Rhyzor stepped into the room, his eyes locking onto hers with that same piercing intensity. The familiar pull between them was there, like gravity, drawing them together. But Kaelith had learned to ignore it, to bury it beneath the weight of her duty. The rebellion had taken everything from her—her peace, her certainty, her sense of control—and now it threatened to take her kingdom. She could not afford to lose herself in anything, anyone. Not even him.

"I need to speak with you," Rhyzor said, his voice low, almost a whisper.

Kaelith nodded, stepping away from the balcony and crossing the room to the table, where maps of the city, battle plans, and reports from the southern districts were spread out in chaotic disarray. The sight of them only deepened the pit in her stomach.

"I've been working with the council," she said, gesturing to the maps. "We've made a plan to repel the rebels from the northern gate. But I need more information from you, Rhyzor. I need to know what we're facing. The Flamebringer—he's more than just a leader. He's a symbol. He's the last of your kind, isn't he?"

Rhyzor's eyes flickered at the mention of the Flamebringer, but he didn't speak right away. He crossed the room, his footsteps soundless, and stood by the window, gazing out into the darkening sky. His back was to her, but Kaelith could feel the weight of his thoughts pressing against her.

"He is not the only one left," Rhyzor said finally, his voice so quiet Kaelith almost didn't hear it. "But he is the most dangerous."

Kaelith's heart quickened. "What does that mean? What are you not telling me?"

Rhyzor turned to face her, his golden eyes gleaming in the dim light. "The Flamebringer—he is my brother."

The words hit Kaelith like a blow. Her breath caught in her throat, and for a moment, the world seemed to spin around her. "Your brother?" she repeated, her voice hoarse with disbelief.

"Yes," Rhyzor said, his jaw tightening. "We were the last of the Rhaedros line. The last of the dragon blood. And when the kingdom fell, when Veyrith's forces slaughtered our people, they left no one alive except for us. Or so I thought."

Kaelith swallowed, her mind racing. She had heard rumors of the dragon bloodline—the ancient, powerful family that had once ruled Rhaedros, a kingdom of dragons and warriors. She had never imagined that Rhyzor's connection to that bloodline went so deep. And now, to hear that his brother—the Flamebringer—was leading the rebellion, threatening everything she had fought for...

"Your brother is leading this war?" Kaelith asked, her voice barely above a whisper.

Rhyzor's gaze hardened. "He is. And he will stop at nothing to see the kingdom fall."

Kaelith stepped closer, her breath catching in her throat. "But why? Why is he doing this? Why attack Veyrith, your own people?"

Rhyzor's eyes seemed to darken, and for a moment, he looked as though he were staring into something distant—something far away. His voice was low, almost pained when he spoke again.

"Because he believes that vengeance is the only thing worth fighting for," Rhyzor said softly. "Because, in his eyes, we were abandoned, betrayed, destroyed by the very people who claimed to be our allies." He met her gaze then, his expression hardening once more. "He doesn't care about the kingdom, Kaelith. He cares only about the blood that was spilled and the destruction of those who took everything from us."

Kaelith felt a pang in her chest, a mixture of sorrow and guilt. She had always known that Rhyzor's people had suffered. She had always known that the destruction of Rhaedros was a tragedy, a consequence of a war that no one had truly understood. But to hear it from Rhyzor himself—to hear the pain in his voice as he spoke of his brother and his people—struck her in a way that words couldn't capture.

"And you?" she asked softly, her heart aching. "What do you want, Rhyzor? What do you want from me?"

For a moment, Rhyzor didn't answer. He simply stood there, his golden eyes fixed on her, as though searching for something—something Kaelith couldn't understand.

"I want to end this," he said at last, his voice raw. "I want to stop the war before it consumes us all. But I cannot do it alone. I need your help, Kaelith."

Kaelith's heart thundered in her chest as she looked at him. She had given him her trust, her alliance, but now, with the weight of his words pressing on her, she realized how little she truly knew about him, about what drove him. His brother. His people. The bloodline that ran through his veins. And now, she stood at the edge of a precipice, the choice before her clearer than ever.

But there was something in Rhyzor's gaze, something that made her hesitate. He was not just a man fighting for vengeance. He was a man who had lost everything. He had been shaped by fire and blood, and the weight of that was too much for any one person to bear alone.

"I will help you," Kaelith said, her voice steady, though her heart pounded in her chest. "But you must understand something, Rhyzor. This—this war—will cost us both. It will cost everything. And when it's over, we will be changed. Both of us."

Rhyzor nodded, his expression softening just slightly. "I understand."

The words hung in the air, and for a moment, Kaelith didn't know if they were talking about the war, or about something much deeper—something neither of them had fully acknowledged. But before she could ask, Rhyzor stepped forward, his hand reaching out for hers. The touch was gentle, a silent promise that neither of them had spoken aloud.

And as his hand brushed against hers, Kaelith felt the weight of the world shift. The kingdom was divided. The rebellion raged on. And in the shadows of war, she had made a choice.

A choice to stand beside the last dragon prince. A choice that would either save her kingdom—or destroy it.

"I don't want to see my people burn," Rhyzor said quietly, his voice a whisper against the howling winds outside. "But I will do whatever it takes to see justice done."

Kaelith squeezed his hand, her voice steady. "Then we will fight together."

And beneath dragon wings, they stood united—not as enemies, but as something new, something forged in the fire of shared loss and ambition. Together, they would face the storm that was coming, knowing that the cost of their choices would be steep. But in the end, they had no choice but to fight.

And so they would. Together.

Sixteen

A Queen's Betrayal

The cold wind howled through the cracks in the palace walls, rattling the windows and sending shivers through the stone halls. Kaelith stood in front of the war table, her back straight, her hands gripping the edges of the map that sprawled before her. The once-sturdy kingdom she had sworn to protect was now splintering before her eyes, and the rebellion she had tried to quell had become a wildfire—untamable, merciless, and closing in on the very heart of Veyrith. The once-proud banners that flew high above the palace now felt like reminders of a past she had been unable to control. Her kingdom was no longer the bastion of strength it had been.

The door to the war room opened with a soft creak, and Kaelith turned, her heart skipping a beat despite herself. General Varek stepped in, his expression grim, his eyes shadowed with the weight of the reports he carried. The usual quiet confidence that defined him was replaced by an edge of frustration—something Kaelith had not seen in him before.

"My queen," Varek said, his voice hoarse, his breath coming in sharp bursts. "I bring news from the council."

Kaelith motioned for him to speak, her mind already racing with the possibilities. The council had been growing restless for days, their demands for action reaching a fever pitch. She had tried to stall them, tried to keep them from making rash decisions, but the situation had become untenable. Every day, the southern districts slipped further from her grasp, and the flames of revolt grew hotter.

"The council has reached a decision," Varek continued, his voice thick with unease. "They are no longer willing to wait. They want to send an army to meet the rebels—no more negotiations, no more delays. They believe that force is the only way to stop them now."

Kaelith's heart sank. The last thing she needed was another war—a war that would tear the kingdom apart. But the council had no patience, no understanding of the delicate balance she had tried to maintain. "They want an attack," Kaelith murmured, her voice barely above a whisper.

Varek nodded, his gaze never leaving hers. "They believe it's our only option, my queen. The Flamebringer is growing stronger, and if we do not strike now, we risk losing everything."

Kaelith closed her eyes for a moment, her fingers brushing the edges of the map. She could feel the pressure mounting, the weight of the crown on her brow. She had already chosen a path. She had aligned herself with Rhyzor, a dangerous alliance that had given her the information she needed to fight the rebellion from within. But that decision had come at a cost. And now, with the council pushing for a military response, she was torn between two paths—the one she had chosen and the one that seemed to be her only remaining option.

"I will not send our people to die for a war we cannot win," Kaelith said, her voice firm. "We will not resort to blind aggression."

Varek's eyes hardened, and for the first time, Kaelith saw the anger that had been simmering beneath his calm exterior. "You are the queen, Kaelith. You must decide. The council will not wait forever. And I do not believe they will listen to you much longer."

Kaelith stood still, her mind racing, her pulse pounding in her ears. The rebellion had already taken its toll on her people, and every day without action made the situation worse. But Rhyzor's words echoed in her mind—This war will cost us both. She had made a pact with him, but every move she made now seemed to drag her deeper into his world—a world where vengeance ruled, and where the flames of war burned hotter with every choice she made.

"I understand," Kaelith said quietly, her voice strained. "I will meet with the council. We will find a way to stop this without bloodshed."

Varek didn't respond immediately. Instead, he stepped closer, his gaze intense. "My queen, I have done everything in my power to support your decisions. But I fear you are playing a dangerous game. You are trusting the very man who is behind the chaos in this kingdom. And we cannot forget that, no matter what promises he has made to you."

Kaelith's chest tightened. She had known this moment would come—the moment when the people she trusted would question her decisions, would question the alliances she had forged. But hearing it from Varek, seeing the doubt in his eyes, made her realize just how fragile everything she had built truly was. She had sworn an oath to Rhyzor, and though that oath had seemed necessary at the time, she could not ignore the doubts that had begun to fester in her mind.

"I made my choice, General," she said, her voice hardening with determination. "And I will stand by it. But I will not sacrifice my people in the process."

Varek bowed his head, his expression unreadable. "As you wish, my queen." He turned and left the room, the door closing softly behind him.

Kaelith remained standing, her hands gripping the edges of the war table as she stared at the maps before her. The council's demands had become impossible to ignore, and Varek's warning echoed in her mind. Rhyzor had become the key to everything—both the answer and the problem. She needed him, but she could not deny the pull of suspicion that now lingered around him like a dark cloud. His motives had always been shrouded in secrecy, and now, with his brother, the Flamebringer, threatening the kingdom, Kaelith found herself questioning everything she had trusted.

And then there was the betrayal.

She could feel it like a knot in her stomach. The council. Varek. They were all pushing her toward war, to act before the rebellion claimed the capital. But they didn't know everything she had learned. They didn't understand the delicate balance she was trying to maintain with Rhyzor. And what if he had lied to her? What if he had used her, played her from the start, knowing she would be the key to bringing his brother down?

No, Kaelith thought firmly. She would not allow her doubts to take control. She had made an oath, and she would keep it. But what she had not counted on—what she had not prepared for—was the betrayal that now lay in wait.

Later that evening, the council gathered in the grand hall, the heavy air thick with uncertainty and anticipation. Kaelith entered the chamber with a sense of calm, her eyes scanning the room as she made her way to the head of the table. The faces of the council members were tense, their expressions unreadable as they waited for her to speak.

Lord Jeren, ever the vocal critic, was the first to speak. "My

A Queen's Betrayal

queen, we have waited long enough. The rebellion has already taken too much from us. We cannot afford to delay any longer."

"I understand the urgency," Kaelith replied evenly, her voice carrying through the room. "But we will not fight blindly. We need to understand the true nature of the rebellion before we send our forces to war."

"And yet," Jeren interjected sharply, "we have no time for such luxuries. The Flamebringer grows stronger every day, and you—" He hesitated for a moment, his voice lowering. "You have been far too cautious. This is not the time for hesitation, Kaelith. You must act now."

"I will act when I know the truth," Kaelith replied, her voice cold, her eyes narrowing. "I will not sacrifice the lives of our people for a war we do not understand."

The room fell silent. The tension was thick, the weight of the council's expectations pressing down on her. But it was not just their gaze that held her in place. It was the knowledge that, beneath all their talk of strategy and war, there was something darker at play—something that threatened to tear her kingdom apart from the inside.

Lord Cailan, ever the opportunist, leaned forward. "Then, my queen, we must ask you a question. What will you do if this rebellion is not so easily stopped? What if you cannot control it? What will you do when the flames of war reach our doorstep?"

Kaelith met his gaze, her eyes cold and steady. "I will do what needs to be done."

Her words hung in the air, a threat wrapped in resolve. She would not let the kingdom burn. Not on her watch.

But as the council began to argue again, Kaelith could not shake the feeling that something had changed. Something darker, more dangerous, was brewing. Rhyzor had already set the wheels in motion, and the rebellion—his rebellion—was no longer something she could control.

In that moment, Kaelith realized the truth: the betrayal had already begun. And it was coming from the one person she had trusted the most.

Seventeen

The Consort's Vow

The wind howled through the palace corridors, carrying with it the scent of rain and the promise of a storm that was not just on the horizon, but deep within the heart of Veyrith. Kaelith stood alone in the war room, the flickering torches casting long shadows that seemed to stretch and bend with the weight of the decisions before her. Her fingers brushed lightly over the map laid out on the table, tracing the lines of the southern districts where the rebellion had taken root, and where the final battle would likely unfold. She could almost hear the distant sounds of war echoing in her mind—clashing swords, the desperate cries of soldiers, the pounding of hooves.

But the most pressing battle she faced wasn't one of strategy or of armies. It was within her own heart. Rhyzor. Her ally. Her consort. The man she had sworn an oath to, the one who had captured her trust and, against all reason, her affection. He had promised to help her end the rebellion. He had promised loyalty, but Kaelith was beginning to wonder if he had ever truly meant those words. She had given him power, allowed him to make decisions alongside her, and yet, as each day passed, she felt the grip of his ambition tightening around her kingdom—and around her heart.

The council had already made its demands clear: act now, or lose everything. Yet Kaelith knew that the stakes were higher than they understood. Rhyzor had been playing a dangerous game, and for the first time, Kaelith could not see the endgame clearly. She had trusted him, given him a platform, a place at her side—and now, the consequences of that trust were spiraling out of control.

The door to the war room opened quietly, and Kaelith didn't need to turn around to know who stood behind her. His presence was unmistakable, a warmth in the coldness of the room.

"You've been avoiding me," Rhyzor's voice cut through the stillness, low and steady, though there was an edge to it that Kaelith had never heard before.

She slowly turned to face him, her hands folding across her chest. "I've been busy," she replied evenly, her voice carrying the weight of her thoughts.

Rhyzor's gaze softened, though the intensity in his eyes remained. He took a step closer, his presence commanding, and for a brief moment, Kaelith felt a pang of uncertainty. "You

The Consort's Vow

should not shut yourself off from me, Kaelith. We need each other more than you realize."

Kaelith's jaw tightened, but she said nothing. Instead, she looked back at the map on the table, tracing the southern border once again. She couldn't ignore the unease that gnawed at her, the sickening feeling that she was no longer in control of the situation. Rhyzor's rebellion had gained more ground, and every time she considered his role in it, her trust wavered.

"You've come to speak of the war," Kaelith said quietly, forcing her voice to remain calm. "The rebellion is pushing toward the capital. The council wants action." She paused, her fingers resting lightly on the edge of the map. "They want us to strike."

"And what do you want?" Rhyzor asked, his voice softer now, but there was something sharp beneath the surface. He had taken a step closer, closing the distance between them, his breath warm against the chill of the room. "Do you want to fight the rebellion as your people demand? Or do you want to face the truth of what we are becoming?"

Kaelith's chest tightened, and she looked up at him, her voice low but filled with a quiet fury. "What are we becoming, Rhyzor?"

He studied her for a long moment, his expression unreadable. "I've given you everything you've asked for, Kaelith. I've trusted you with my heart, my people, my blood. I've stood by you when others would have turned away." His voice dropped, becoming colder. "And yet, you question my loyalty? You doubt the vow

I made to you?"

Kaelith's heart skipped, a mixture of guilt and anger rising in her chest. She had trusted him. She had brought him into her world, into her kingdom, and allowed him to share power. But now, every decision, every move he made felt like a manipulation. His words, his promises—they had seemed so genuine, so sincere, and now, they twisted in her mind. Had she been a fool? Had she been blind to the truth?

"You promised me you would help me end the rebellion," Kaelith said, her voice steady but filled with the weight of her emotions. "But I never asked you to take control of it. I never asked you to make the choices you've made."

Rhyzor's eyes narrowed, his jaw tightening as though he were fighting to control himself. "You think I've taken control?" His voice was sharp now, the restraint gone. "You think I've made decisions without you? Without us?" He stepped forward, his presence overwhelming. "I have fought for you, Kaelith. I've fought for the future of this kingdom. And yet you doubt me at every turn."

Kaelith's throat constricted as he moved closer, his voice low and dangerous. "You think this is a game, Rhyzor?" She stepped back, her gaze never leaving his. "You think I don't see what you're doing?"

Rhyzor's eyes darkened, his expression hardening. "I have given you everything. I've given you power, my loyalty, my heart. And this is how you repay me?"

The words struck her like a blow. For the first time, she saw the full extent of his anger, the depth of his control over her. He had manipulated her trust, used her need for an alliance to further his own goals. But she had not seen it—she had been too blinded by the promise of victory, by the hope that this war could be won without more bloodshed.

"I never asked you for this," Kaelith said quietly, her voice trembling with the weight of her realization. "I never asked you to stake everything on this rebellion. I thought we were allies. But I've been wrong. I've been wrong about everything."

Rhyzor's expression softened, but the hardness in his eyes remained. He reached out, his hand brushing against hers, but Kaelith recoiled instinctively. She could feel the pull of his touch, the warmth of his body, but it was no longer comforting. It was suffocating.

"You say you're wrong, Kaelith," he said, his voice almost too soft, too dangerous. "But you've never truly trusted me. Not in the way I trust you. Not in the way we need each other to survive this."

Kaelith stood still, her heart pounding in her chest, her mind a whirlwind of confusion. She had come so far, had made so many sacrifices, but now, she saw it—she saw the truth of her mistake. She had allowed herself to be manipulated, to be swept away by the promises of a man who had never truly been loyal to her cause. And now, that betrayal was unfolding before her eyes, as if it had been there all along, hidden in plain sight.

"I trusted you," Kaelith said quietly, her voice barely a whisper. "And you have betrayed me."

Rhyzor took a step back, his eyes widening with surprise, but he quickly masked it with a cruel smile. "Betrayal? Perhaps. But it is not you who has been betrayed, Kaelith. It is me. I have given everything to this kingdom, to you. I have sacrificed my people, my birthright, all for the promise of a future that I thought we could build together. And now, you question me?" His voice hardened with fury. "I have given you my loyalty, my heart, and my soul. What more could you ask for?"

Kaelith's chest tightened, the weight of his words crashing down on her. She had trusted him, yes. But she had also trusted herself to make the right decisions. And now, she realized with a sickening clarity, that she had allowed herself to be blinded by the very thing she had vowed to protect: power.

"I will not be controlled," Kaelith said, her voice rising with the strength of her resolve. "I will not allow you to use me or this kingdom for your vengeance."

Rhyzor's gaze softened, but there was a coldness beneath it. "Vengeance is what this kingdom has always been built on, Kaelith. It is what will tear us apart, or what will save us." He reached out once again, but this time, Kaelith stepped back, shaking her head.

"No," she said, her voice firm and resolute. "You have made your choices, Rhyzor. And I have made mine."

She turned away from him, her heart pounding in her chest, the weight of her decision settling on her like a stone. She had chosen the kingdom. She had chosen the people who had once stood by her side, and she had chosen the path of survival—not the path of revenge.

Rhyzor's voice was cold as he spoke, his words cutting through the tension in the room. "Then we are done, Kaelith. I am done with you. You will see the consequences of your choices."

Kaelith didn't turn back. She couldn't. She had made the vow. And now, she would face the consequences of breaking it.

The kingdom was divided. And the storm that had been building for so long was about to break.

Eighteen

The Battle of Fire and Blood

The first light of dawn had barely broken over the horizon, casting an eerie red glow over the capital. The sky was thick with the smoke of the city's defenses—torches blazing along the walls, the scent of burning wood mingling with the sharp tang of fear that hung heavy in the air. Kaelith stood at the edge of the battlements, her gaze fixed on the distant hills where the rebellion was gathering. Her heart raced, the tension in her chest tightening with each passing moment. The time for diplomacy, for negotiations, had passed. Today, the fate of her kingdom would be decided.

Behind her, the war room was quiet. The council had finally agreed to her plan—no more delays, no more waiting. The rebels, led by the Flamebringer, had crossed the southern border and were marching toward the capital. It was no longer a matter of finding a peaceful resolution. It was a matter of survival. The capital was surrounded, the walls were ready to be breached, and the soldiers had gathered. The battle was coming.

And at the heart of it, was Rhyzor.

Kaelith's thoughts were clouded with uncertainty as she gripped the stone railing, the wind biting at her skin. Rhyzor had promised her the rebellion would end, but the cost of that promise had already begun to reveal itself. Their alliance had been a gamble, and Kaelith was beginning to wonder if it had been one she could never win.

"My queen," Varek's voice broke through her thoughts, steady and calm, though there was a trace of worry in his tone.

Kaelith turned to face him. The general's eyes were sharp, his face drawn with the fatigue of the long nights they had spent preparing for the inevitable. "It's time," she said, her voice hollow, her eyes distant.

"We've prepared as much as we can," Varek replied, his voice tight with the weight of responsibility. "The southern districts are lost, and the enemy is closing in. We can only hold the gates for so long."

Kaelith nodded slowly, her heart heavy with the knowledge that they were out of options. The council was demanding a decisive strike, and the people were waiting for her to lead them. She had always known the price of the crown would be high, but today, the cost seemed insurmountable. "What of

Rhyzor?" she asked, her voice strained with a question she had been avoiding.

Varek's expression darkened, and he looked away for a moment before meeting her gaze. "He's gone."

Kaelith's breath caught in her throat. "Gone?"

"He left the palace last night," Varek continued, his voice low. "No one saw him leave, but the soldiers report that he has joined the Flamebringer's forces. He's betrayed you, my queen."

A coldness settled over Kaelith, and for a moment, the world seemed to blur around her. She had suspected it, feared it even, but hearing it aloud was like a punch to the gut. Rhyzor—her consort, her ally—had turned against her. The man she had trusted with the kingdom was now leading the very forces that threatened to destroy it.

The betrayal stung more than she had expected. It wasn't just a matter of politics or power—it was personal. Rhyzor had promised her he would help her end the rebellion. He had sworn loyalty to her. And now, as the battle for the capital loomed, he had sided with the enemy.

"Prepare the soldiers," Kaelith said, her voice steady, though her heart ached. "We fight for Veyrith."

Varek hesitated for a moment, his gaze searching hers. "Are you sure, my queen? We can still turn back. We can negotiate—"

The Battle of Fire and Blood

"No." Kaelith's voice was firm, resolute. "The time for negotiation is over. We will fight. And we will win."

Varek bowed his head, his expression grim. "As you command, my queen."

The battle for the capital began just before noon, when the first wave of rebels arrived at the city gates. The ground shook with the pounding of hooves, the air filled with the cries of battle. Kaelith stood at the head of her forces, the weight of the crown on her brow heavier than ever before. The soldiers, her people, stood behind her, their faces grim but determined. They had no choice now but to fight.

Kaelith could feel the tension in the air, the electricity of war crackling around her. The capital was her home, her kingdom, her heart. And she would protect it, no matter the cost.

"We must hold the gates," Varek shouted to the soldiers beside him, his voice rising above the din of the battlefield. "If the rebels breach the walls, we are lost!"

Kaelith's eyes scanned the horizon, watching as the first wave of the enemy forces approached. She could see them now, a sea of soldiers, their banners flying high. The Flamebringer was at their head, his figure unmistakable—a shadow against the rising smoke, a figure of power and destruction.

And there, beside him, was Rhyzor. His dark figure stood tall among the rebels, his eyes gleaming with determination as he led them toward the city. For a moment, Kaelith's heart faltered. The sight of him—standing with the very enemy she had sworn to defeat—felt like a knife to her soul.

But there was no time for hesitation. There was no time for doubt.

"Archers!" Varek shouted, his voice ringing out like a command from the gods. "Fire!"

The archers, stationed on the walls, drew their bows and released a volley of arrows into the air, sending a rain of sharp steel toward the oncoming enemy. The arrows fell like a storm, cutting through the ranks of the rebels. But the Flamebringer's forces were relentless, and for every rebel that fell, another took their place. The battle had begun in earnest, and there would be no turning back.

Kaelith's eyes narrowed as she watched the chaos unfold. The city was under siege, the gates were holding—for now—but she could feel the pressure building. The weight of the battle pressed down on her like a mountain, and yet, she stood firm. She was the queen. And she would not let her people fall.

"Send in the cavalry," Kaelith ordered, her voice unwavering despite the rising panic in her chest. "We push them back."

The cavalry charged from the rear, their hooves thundering against the ground as they joined the fray. The clash of steel rang out as the soldiers met in brutal combat. Kaelith fought to

The Battle of Fire and Blood

keep her mind clear, focusing on the movements of her troops, watching as the enemy pushed ever closer. Her heart beat in time with the rhythm of the war, and she could feel the storm of battle consuming everything.

But even as the battle raged, Kaelith couldn't shake the feeling that something was wrong. The rebels were too coordinated, too strategic. It was as if they had known exactly when and where to strike.

And then she saw him.

Rhyzor. Standing at the front of the rebel army, his sword drawn, his eyes locked onto hers across the battlefield. For a moment, the world seemed to pause—his gaze cutting through the chaos as if it were meant only for her.

"Rhyzor," she whispered to herself, her heart heavy with the weight of everything that had brought her to this point. He was no longer just an enemy. He was a symbol of everything she had lost.

The Flamebringer raised his hand, signaling a charge. The rebels surged forward, crashing against the gates with an intensity that threatened to tear them apart. Kaelith's soldiers fought valiantly, but the enemy was relentless.

"Push them back!" Varek shouted, his voice hoarse with the strain of command. "We can't let them breach the gates!"

But the rebels were too strong. The walls trembled under the weight of their assault, and Kaelith could hear the sound of splintering wood as the gate began to crack.

The cavalry had taken a heavy toll, but there were too many rebels now. They were pushing through, overwhelming her forces, breaking through the walls like a flood. The battle was slipping from her grasp.

Kaelith's breath caught in her throat as she saw the Flamebringer raise his sword high, his eyes gleaming with bloodlust. He was so close now—so close to the gates, so close to victory. But it was Rhyzor who caught her gaze again, his eyes filled with something darker, something colder.

Her heart twisted with pain as she saw the truth in his eyes—he had never truly been on her side. He had never truly been loyal to her or her kingdom.

And in that moment, Kaelith knew: there would be no peace, no resolution. The Flamebringer was the end. And Rhyzor—the man she had trusted—was the beginning of her kingdom's fall.

"Fall back!" she screamed, her voice rising above the chaos. "We cannot hold them!"

But it was too late.

The gates finally gave way, crashing to the ground with a deafening roar. The rebels poured through, their battle cries echoing in the air like thunder. The battle of fire and blood had come to an end—but the war was just beginning.

Nineteen

The Price of Love

The night had fallen heavily over Veyrith, a blanket of darkness that seemed to smother the city in its cold embrace. The once-bustling streets were now eerily silent, the sounds of battle having subsided, leaving only the distant echoes of cries and the clamor of soldiers as they regrouped in the city's shattered defenses. The gates had been breached, and the enemy had poured through, tearing apart what little had been left standing. It was a victory, but not the one Kaelith had hoped for.

The palace, once a symbol of power and security, now felt like a prison, its walls closing in on her. Kaelith paced back and forth in the war room, the weight of her decisions bearing down on her like an anchor. The rebellion had succeeded in taking the city, and Rhyzor had led the charge. He had betrayed her, and with that betrayal came the crumbling of everything she had worked for.

Her breath came in shallow bursts, the air thick with the stench of smoke and blood that seemed to cling to her skin. The room was dimly lit, the flickering candles casting long shadows on the walls. She could hear the distant sounds of soldiers gathering, preparing for the final push, but they felt like a world away. Her mind was racing, filled with thoughts of Rhyzor, of the war, of the kingdom she had lost. She had never imagined that the price of love would be so high, that the cost of trusting someone so deeply would ultimately be the destruction of everything she held dear.

The door to the war room creaked open, and Kaelith turned sharply, her heart racing. Her pulse quickened as she saw who stood in the doorway. It was him—Rhyzor.

He was drenched in blood, his armor torn, his face streaked with dirt and sweat. He looked every bit the conqueror he had become, and yet, in his eyes, Kaelith saw something else. There was no joy in his victory. No satisfaction in the bloodshed he had caused. His expression was empty, hollow, as though something inside of him had died along with the kingdom.

"You're here," Kaelith said, her voice barely more than a whisper. She didn't know whether she was relieved, angry, or terrified. Perhaps she was all three.

Rhyzor stepped into the room, his gaze never leaving hers. His jaw was clenched, his posture tense as if he were preparing for something—something far more dangerous than the battle outside. He took a step forward, but Kaelith didn't move. She couldn't. Her body felt as though it were made of stone, her limbs frozen by the weight of his presence.

"I came because I had to," Rhyzor said, his voice low and rough, as though speaking took all of his strength. "Because you wanted me to, remember?"

Kaelith's breath caught in her throat. She had wanted him to help her, to end the rebellion. She had believed in him, trusted him with her kingdom, her heart. But now, as she looked at him—really looked at him—she saw only the man who had betrayed her. The man who had brought the fire, the blood, and the chaos that now consumed everything she loved.

"You betrayed me," Kaelith said, her voice hardening with each word. "You promised me that we would end this rebellion together, that we would save this kingdom. And yet, here we are. You led your army into my capital, my people—" She stopped, her chest tightening as the words caught in her throat.

Rhyzor's expression flickered for a moment, as though he were about to say something—something that might explain it all. But instead, he stepped closer, his presence overwhelming. He didn't speak at first, but his gaze never left hers, as if trying to reach some deeper part of her that had yet to understand.

"I never meant for it to happen this way," he said quietly, his voice breaking slightly. "You think I wanted this? You think I wanted to bring war to your doorstep?" He exhaled sharply, frustration creeping into his voice. "I didn't want any of this,

The Price of Love

Kaelith. You have to understand. This was never about the kingdom—it was about vengeance. About making them pay for what they did to us."

Kaelith's mind spun, the words crashing into her like waves. Vengeance. It had always been about vengeance. But what did that mean for her? What did it mean for the kingdom they had both built and destroyed together?

"Vengeance?" Kaelith repeated, her voice tinged with disbelief. "You killed my people. You tore apart the very fabric of what I swore to protect." Her voice faltered, and she clenched her fists at her sides, fighting back the tears that threatened to break free. "You took everything from me, Rhyzor. Everything."

Rhyzor stepped forward, his hand reaching for her, but Kaelith pulled away, taking a step back, her chest heaving with the force of her emotions. She couldn't let him touch her. Not now. Not after everything.

"I had to do it," he said, his voice raw. "You think I didn't feel every moment of it? Every death? Every broken promise? I've lived with the pain of my people's slaughter for years, Kaelith. I've carried it inside me, waiting for the moment when I could make it right. When I could make them pay."

Kaelith's vision blurred, the anger rising in her chest, but it was tempered by something deeper. Something that made her falter. It was pain. She could see the pain in his eyes, the torment that twisted his features, and it made her doubt everything she had believed. Was it possible that he, too, was just a man broken by the world, a man who had lost everything, just as she had?

"You think I don't understand pain?" Kaelith whispered, her voice cracking. "You think I don't know what it's like to lose everything? To watch your world burn around you? I lost my mother. I lost my father. I lost my people, Rhyzor. And yet, I didn't choose vengeance. I chose this kingdom. I chose to rebuild it." She shook her head, a bitter laugh escaping her lips. "But you? You chose fire. You chose destruction."

The silence that hung between them was deafening. Kaelith could feel the weight of their history pressing down on her—years of unspoken words, of dreams destroyed, of broken promises. They were both lost in their own ways, but there was no going back now.

"I didn't want this, Kaelith," Rhyzor said, his voice softer now, almost pleading. "I didn't want to destroy what we had. But I couldn't live with the lies anymore. I couldn't pretend that everything was fine, that we could just move on from the past." He reached out again, his hand trembling. "I loved you, Kaelith. I still do."

The words hit her like a storm, and for a moment, her heart skipped a beat. She could see it in his eyes—the same thing she had seen when they were younger, the same longing, the same pain. The love that had once burned so brightly between them now felt like a distant memory, a flickering light in the darkness.

But love was not enough. Not anymore.

The Price of Love

"Love?" Kaelith whispered, her voice trembling with a mix of grief and anger. "You don't understand what love is. You used me. You played me, and you knew it. You never cared about the kingdom. You never cared about the people. All you wanted was revenge."

Rhyzor's expression faltered, his face a mixture of anguish and regret. "I didn't mean to hurt you, Kaelith," he said softly. "I never wanted to hurt you." He stepped closer, but Kaelith backed away again, her breath shallow.

"Then why did you betray me?" Kaelith demanded, her voice thick with emotion. "Why did you turn against me, against everything we fought for?"

Rhyzor stood still for a long moment, his gaze searching hers, and for a brief moment, Kaelith saw the man she had once known—the man who had loved her, the man who had fought beside her. But that man was gone, swallowed up by the flames of vengeance, by the war he had chosen.

"I thought you understood," he whispered. "I thought you'd see that it was never about the kingdom. It was about us. It was about what was taken from us."

Kaelith shook her head, her chest tight with the weight of her decision. "I can't forgive you, Rhyzor. I can't forgive what you've done. Not now. Not ever."

Rhyzor looked down, a slow, resigned breath escaping his lips. "Then I have lost you," he said quietly, his voice barely audible.

"I have lost everything."

The room seemed to grow colder, the weight of his words hanging heavy in the air. Kaelith stood firm, her heart breaking in two. But the woman she had become—strong, resolute, a queen—could not afford to be swayed by his tears, by his regrets.

"You lost me the moment you chose this path," Kaelith said, her voice steady despite the storm in her chest. "And now, the price of love is the price of everything we've lost. You have lost your kingdom, Rhyzor. And I have lost you."

With that, she turned away, the finality of her words hanging in the air. She could feel Rhyzor's gaze burning into her back as she walked away, her heart heavy with the weight of the truth she had finally accepted.

Love, it seemed, was the price of everything. And in the end, Kaelith realized, it was not worth the cost.

Twenty

The Rise of the Dragon Queen

The sky was darkening, the once-clear blue marred by the heavy clouds that had gathered overhead. The city of Veyrith, its cobbled streets and towering spires, stood beneath the oppressive weight of an impending storm. The winds were picking up, whipping through the broken gates and scattered banners, carrying with them the promise of change. As the sun dipped beneath the horizon, casting the city in a twilight haze, Kaelith stood in the courtyard, her hands clenched tightly around the hilt of her sword.

The battle had raged for days, the rebellion moving ever closer to victory. Her forces had been stretched thin, the city's defenses weakening under the constant onslaught. And yet, even as she stood on the edge of defeat, Kaelith felt something stirring deep within her—a fire that had lain dormant for far too long.

Her heart beat with the weight of her decisions. The betrayal of Rhyzor. The fall of the kingdom. And yet, amid the destruction and despair, Kaelith knew one thing for certain: she would not surrender. She would not let Veyrith fall.

The clattering of footsteps echoed from behind her, and Kaelith turned, her eyes sharp as she saw Varek approach. His expression was grave, his eyes dark with the knowledge of the situation. The time for diplomacy had long since passed. Now, it was only a matter of survival.

"My queen," Varek said, his voice low and filled with the urgency of the moment. "The rebels have breached the outer walls. We cannot hold them back much longer."

Kaelith's jaw tightened, her gaze fixed on the horizon. The distant sound of battle reached her ears—shouts, the clash of metal, the screams of the wounded. Her people were fighting, but they were losing. They had always been outnumbered, outmatched by the sheer strength of the rebellion. But there was something else. The heart of the rebellion—the one that had brought her to this point—was no longer just the Flamebringer. It was Rhyzor.

He had betrayed her, but more than that, he had become something else. He was the embodiment of everything that had been lost, and now, he led the very force that threatened to destroy all she had worked for.

"I know," Kaelith said quietly, her voice tinged with sorrow, but also determination. "But we will fight. We will hold the line until the last. This city will not fall without a fight."

Varek's face softened, his gaze filled with concern. "My queen, the rebellion is not just at the gates. It's inside these walls. We have spies—those loyal to the Flamebringer—working in the shadows. We cannot trust anyone, not even within our own ranks."

Kaelith nodded, her mind racing. The web of betrayal had grown far more tangled than she had ever imagined. Her kingdom, once a beacon of strength and unity, had been corrupted from within. But there was one thing left that they could count on—her.

"Gather the troops," Kaelith commanded. "We are not done yet. I will lead them into the heart of the battle. If we must fall, we will fall with honor."

Varek bowed low, his expression one of silent respect. "As you wish, my queen." He turned to leave but stopped at the door, casting one last glance at her. "Be careful, Kaelith. You do not need to carry this burden alone."

"I know," Kaelith replied, her voice softening for just a moment. "But it's my fight now. And I will not back down."

With that, Varek exited, leaving Kaelith alone in the courtyard. The sound of the battle grew louder, but Kaelith stood still, allowing the weight of the moment to settle over her. Her people were dying, and yet, she could not afford to let them see her falter. She was their queen. She had made a vow, not just to them, but to herself. This was her kingdom. And she would not let it be destroyed by the flames of vengeance.

Her thoughts drifted back to Rhyzor—the man who had once stood at her side, the man who had shared her dreams of a united kingdom. The man who had promised her loyalty, only to turn against her. The man who had made her believe that there was something more between them—a bond that could never be broken.

But she had been wrong. Rhyzor was no longer the man she had once known. He was a symbol of everything she had fought against. And in his eyes, she had seen it—something darker, something that could never be undone. He was her greatest mistake, her greatest betrayal. But even that, Kaelith knew, could not stop her from doing what she had to do.

She had given him power. She had trusted him. And now, the price of that trust was the very kingdom they had both claimed to love.

But Kaelith was done with doubt. She was done with hesitation. It was time to rise.

The city was on fire.

Kaelith stood at the gates, her armor gleaming in the dim light of the burning city. The soldiers lined up behind her, their faces set with grim determination. The ground beneath their feet shook with the force of the advancing rebels. Her forces were few—too few—but they would fight until the last. The city's walls had been breached, and now, it was a fight to the death.

Kaelith's hand rested on the hilt of her sword, the blade cold beneath her fingers. Her heart was steady now, her resolve unwavering. This was the moment she had been preparing for. The final stand.

"Hold the line!" Kaelith shouted, her voice carrying across the battlefield. The soldiers around her raised their weapons in unison, their roars of defiance echoing through the air.

Ahead of them, the Flamebringer and his army were marching toward the gates, the ground trembling beneath their footsteps. Kaelith could see Rhyzor now, standing at the front of his forces, his eyes locked on her across the distance. His armor was black, his sword raised high in a signal to his army. He was no longer the man she had once known. He was a conqueror, a general of an army that sought nothing less than the destruction of everything Kaelith held dear.

"Today, we fight for our kingdom!" Kaelith cried, her voice rising with the fury of a thousand storms. "Today, we fight for our future!"

The soldiers roared in response, their voices shaking the very earth beneath them. Kaelith could feel the fire in her veins, the heat of the battle filling her with a strange sense of purpose. This was it. This was the moment that would define her. Whether she lived or died, she would not let the kingdom fall.

The clash of steel rang out as the enemy advanced, the battle beginning in a roar of fury and violence. The ground was slick with blood as the two armies collided, soldiers from both sides fighting desperately for survival. The gates were holding, but just barely.

Kaelith led her soldiers into the fray, her sword flashing through the air as she cut down one rebel after another. Her heart was a drumbeat in her chest, each strike, each blow, a reminder of everything she was fighting for. She could feel the presence of the Flamebringer ahead of her, could feel his gaze on her, but she could not afford to think of him now. There was no room for doubt, no time for hesitation.

The battle raged on, the rebels pressing harder and harder against the gates. Kaelith could see the soldiers around her faltering, their faces drawn with exhaustion and fear. But she refused to let them break. She refused to let them fall.

And then, she saw him.

Rhyzor.

He was standing at the edge of the battlefield, his eyes fixed on her, his sword raised high. The Flamebringer was not far behind, leading his forces toward the heart of the city. Kaelith's breath caught in her throat as their gazes locked. For a moment, the chaos of the battlefield fell away, and she saw only him—the man she had loved, the man who had betrayed her, the man who now stood against her.

"You," Kaelith whispered, her heart aching with the weight of it all.

Rhyzor's lips curled into a smile, but it was cold, distant. "It was never about you, Kaelith. It was never about your kingdom." He raised his sword, his voice carrying across the battlefield. "It's about vengeance. And you chose the wrong side."

Kaelith's grip tightened on her sword, her anger rising like a storm. "I chose the side of my people, Rhyzor. You chose the side of destruction."

With a roar, Rhyzor charged toward her, his army following in his wake. The battle surged forward once more, and Kaelith met him in the center of the battlefield, their swords clashing with a thunderous sound.

For a moment, everything slowed, the world narrowing to just the two of them. Rhyzor's eyes were filled with fire, but Kaelith saw something else there too—regret, pain, a hint of something that still connected them, no matter how far apart they had drifted.

"I'll stop you, Kaelith," Rhyzor said, his voice low and filled with rage. "I'll stop everything you've built. I'll burn it all to the ground."

Kaelith's heart shattered with the weight of his words, but she could not falter. She would not falter.

"I will stop you," Kaelith said, her voice firm, her resolve solid.

"I will save my people. And I will make sure you never burn anything again."

The clash of swords continued, a battle of fire and blood that would decide the fate of a kingdom. And as the flames of war roared around her, Kaelith knew that this was the moment of her rise. She would stand tall, no matter what came next.

She would rise. And she would fight.

www.ingramcontent.com/pod-product-compliance
Lightning Source LLC
LaVergne TN
LVHW010224070526
838199LV00062B/4721